A MINSTREL'S ♫ NOTES ♫

I0087559

♪ STORIES AND SERMONS ON ♪

WORSHIP IN SPIRIT AND IN TRUTH
AND

MUSIC THEORY AND TECHNIQUE
FOR THE ACOUSTIC GUITAR:

Music Notation, Chord Patterns,
Diatonic Scale Patterns,
Finger Picking Patterns.
Practice Tips For Improvisation
and Accompaniment

"BUT NOW BRING ME A MINSTREL . . .

II Kings 3:15

JOHN JAY FRANK

A MINSTREL'S
NOTES

STORIES AND SERMONS ON
WORSHIP IN SPIRIT AND IN TRUTH
AND
MUSIC THEORY AND TECHNIQUE
FOR THE ACOUSTIC GUITAR:

Music Notation, Chord Patterns,
Diatonic Scale Patterns,
Finger Picking Patterns.
Practice Tips For Improvisation
and Accompaniment,

Copyright 1995 Revised 2018
JOHN JAY FRANK

ISBN 1-887835-11-3
9781887835114

Published by Minstrel Missions LLC.
Contact: minstrelmissions@gmail.com
www.minstrelmissions.com

* * * * * * * *

Contents

These notes make up a symphony on worship. Some are old and some new (Matt 13:52). Some of these notes discuss values, or standards of worth which can be debated. Others hit major highs and some, like the minstrel nightmares, sound a more somber, serious, minor tone. Each one, written separately, can stand by itself. There remains many variations to explore around this theme.

Part II - Music Theory and Technique For The Acoustic Guitar
pg. 55 - 83

Introduction

This collection of notes on worship in Spirit and in Truth includes several short stories from a variety of sources, recast and modified to fit this topic. Also included are some general music and church themes This book will explore who, how, why, when, and where we worship and the meaning of prophetic worship. Here are some scriptures to begin the exploration:

You shall have no other gods before me.
  Exodus 20:3, and Deuteronomy 5:7.

Do not worship the Lord your God in the way these pagan people worship their gods. Deuteronomy 12:4.

God is a Spirit: and they that worship him must worship him in spirit and in truth. John 4:24.

Be filled with the Spirit; Speaking to yourselves in psalms, hymns and spiritual songs, singing and making melody in your heart to the Lord; Giving thanks always for all things unto God and the Father in the name of our Lord Jesus Christ. Ephesians 5:18-20.

Worship God: for the testimony of Jesus is the spirit of prophecy.
Revelation 19:10.

* * * * * * * *

Guitar playing has been one of my main activities for over thirty years. Much of that time has been spent leading or accompanying worship. Over the years I recorded the songs the Lord has given me, as well as many hymns, carols, choruses, and classical guitar music. I also use the guitar as a pulpit to preach the gospel. My recordings of original songs are best described as musical sermons or ballads. It should come as no surprise therefore, that when putting together my notes on guitar playing for students, I would also use the opportunity to preach and teach a little about worship.

As a traveling minstrel I have been blessed with access to churches and home groups of all types where I enjoy the worship and the fellowship. I get to spend quality time with pastors and worship leaders and listen to their stories and share some of my own. Some of those are in this book. However, the focus of this book would best be labeled as **intimate and prophetic worship**. That is where my heart's desire is. ***Worship for me is fellowship and communion with God.*** Here are three introductory stories I modified to this topic to help set the tone.

1)   The Lord came by to visit three worshipers. The organist He listened to from a distance. Every now and then He would smile and nod His head. When He got to the piano player He went over, shook hands and gave a reassuring pat on the back. The guitarist He threw His arms around, hugged, kissed, lifted up, danced with, and in general made a big fuss over. Who of the three was more dear to the Lord? Who was the most mature? Who was the most spiritual or the better worshiper?

The one who got the most attention? Perhaps not. How do we act when we come upon a baby or young child? Isn't it more like the third scene than the first? When visiting a mature son going about the Father's business, or a son who is just beginning the work, the relationship may seem more like scene number one or two above. What we consider to be "enthusiastic" worship may not be a sign of depth or maturity. We just may be at an age where we *need* more of God's presence or encouragement!

I was born again in the fires of a Holy Ghost revival and renewal. I do not apologize for that, but neither do I vaunt it. I am a sinner saved by grace. The Lord has shown me the lives and hearts of many who love Him, but who do not engage in the sort of Spiritual manifestations which I consider normal. These include Holy Spirit manifestations, as well as singing songs more than once, perhaps even dozens of times, shouting, clapping, dancing, leaping, running, or in other words, "worshiping God with the whole body, soul, and spirit."

The things shared in the book are not meant to cast doubts about someone's "Spirituality" or relationship with God. It is hoped that it will help increase faith, and increase the hunger and thirst for God. *We all need more of God!*

2)   The book of Judges tells the stories of the battles and the conquest of the kingdom by the people of Israel. They asked "who shall go up for us first? The Lord said, Judah shall go up: behold: I have delivered the land into his hand. Judah shall go up first." (Judges 1: 1-2). Judah, in Hebrew, means praise. Throughout the Bible we see examples of praise and worship to our God leading the way as God's people more fully experience and possess that which He has provided for them. Jehoshaphat even had the musicians march in front of the army (II Chron. 20:21)!

In the New Testament we hear of the worship by Mary when told of her role, the worship by men and angels when Jesus was born, the adoration at his resurrection, the rejoicing at the first Pentecost, or when even one sinner gets saved. The Bible tells us, in the last days, the final separation is between those whose main focus in life indicates that they worship the Lord and those who do not (Rev. 13:4). There is also a difference between the songs sung by those who are saved, and by those who follow Christ most closely (Rev. 19:1, 14:3, & 15:3). Worship is a major aspect of our faith, our life, our relation to God, our walk with Jesus, and our relationship with other Christians.

3)   Another story can be found in nature. The great coral reefs are teeming with life. The living coral itself is just a thin layer on top. What they produce, the beautiful rock-like structures, are the homes and place of sustenance for a multitude of God's creatures.

Worship, especially true prophetic worship, may lead the way, begin the battle, or provide the structure for other things. Worship that is full of Spiritual life produces much beyond the worship service itself. With it, a church building becomes a sanctuary, a holy place of inspiration for the many membered body of Christ, each providing to one another that portion we have been gifted with. We are connected to each other by one Spirit, one Word, one faith, one God. It is God who, by His grace, distributes as He wills, both natural talents or supernatural gifts so we all may fellowship with Him now and in eternity (Matt. 25:15, I Cor. 12:11-27).

* * * * * * *

You also, as lively stones, are built up a spiritual house, an holy priesthood, to offer up spiritual sacrifices, acceptable to God by Jesus Christ. But you *are* a chosen generation, a royal priesthood, an holy nation, a peculiar people; that ye should shew forth the praises of him who hath called you out of darkness into his marvelous light: 1 Peter 2: 5, 9.

Pass On The Promise
by John Jay Frank

Adam said to Seth his son; "God promised to my wife,"
And Abraham told Isaac too; "God has a sacrifice,"
And Jacob knew he'd come back home, even after life.
They all were mighty witnesses, passing on the light.

Moses said to Joshua; "it's now your turn to lead,"
As Samuel anointed king David and his seed,
While Elisha clung to Elijah's side for the mantle he would need,
And with that cloud of witnesses, we will one day be.

Pass on the promise pass the faith, the mantle and the flame,
And pass the courage, pass the hope, for this battle has its pain,
Pass on the power of His love, His nature and His name,
Then join that cloud of witnesses for whom Lord Jesus came.

From Matthew, Mark, to Luke, and John, the Gospel passes on,
The manger, the cross, the empty tomb, the King returning soon,
A vision of the bride to be, the marriage of the Lamb,
The city of our God restored, fulfillment of His plan.

Pass on the promise pass the faith, the mantle and the flame,
And pass the courage, pass the hope, for this battle has its pain,
When you've fought your fight and won your race, the victory's assured,
Then join that cloud of witnesses, returning with our Lord,
That mighty cloud of witnesses, returning with our Lord.

This song was given to me by the Lord while I was beginning language study. I received a phone call telling me a dear saint, Edgar Parkins, a retired missionary and one of my Bible teachers, had gone on to be with the Lord. As I grieved and cried at the news and the "temporary" loss, it seemed as though a tongue of fire wrote this view from eternity across my forehead. I prayed for the music and the Lord gave that too.

Not every song I write comes with such a strong witness, but if the Lord is not in it, I do not sing it. Sometimes I sense His presence at the beginning, and sometimes only later, after prayer and spending time with the words. It can take time to understand what a song means, and at times just a little change in the words is all it takes to make a song worth singing and sharing.

I - The Attributes Of Deity
- Who We Worship

Some folks became irate, bent out of shape, and all riled up when they heard the question, "Can God make a rock which is too heavy for him to move?" For many, it sounds like foolish philosophy. Another, similar question is, "If a tree falls in a forest, and nobody is near enough to hear it, does it make a sound?" A third question to go along with those two is, "how many angels can dance on the head of a pin?" Are these just the stuff of man's vain, empty imagination? What do they have to do with worship? They have to do with *who* we worship. They are specific questions about the nature of God.

The first challenges God's omnipotence (He is all powerful), the second His omniscience (He is all knowing), and the third questions His omnipresence (He is everywhere present). Christians should have no problem recognizing and presenting the One we worship. He is the only true God who is **all powerful** and **all knowing**. Although He chose to manifest Himself in the person of His Son, Jesus Christ, He is also **always and everywhere present**. These are the attributes of Deity of the One: Father, Son, and Holy Spirit, the Three-in-One God who we worship. These attributes of God are so unique, some folks just have a hard time believing in God.

Is God powerful enough to make something which that same power cannot move. He certainly is. There is no contradiction about it. We can find the answer in the Bible of course. Psalm 138 verse 2 says "I will worship toward thy holy temple, and praise thy name for thy loving-kindness and for thy truth: **for thou hast magnified thy word above all thy name**. The name of God includes all those attributes of unlimited power and ability. However, God Himself has decreed that no one may come to Him, no salvation is possible, except by faith in Jesus Christ - who is the Word of God (Jn. 1:14, Acts 4:12). God has limited His ability to move and save anyone in any way at all. He has placed that Rock, Christ Jesus above His name. Jesus was not created of course He was begotten, sent forth, and because of His obedience unto death on the cross, God magnified His Word (Jesus) above His name (Almighty). Jesus, who is all God and all man, is made to the world the only way to God. That Rock cannot be moved (Matt. 19:26) and God is still all powerful.

The second question invites us to look into our definition of sound and how we know something to be true. With this we easily fall into the trap of self-centeredness. It may be a surprise to some people, but mankind is not the center of the universe nor do we define truth or the ultimate reality. The word of God is more trustworthy.

Jesus said in Matt. 10:29-31, "Are not two sparrows sold for a farthing and one of them shall not fall to the ground without your Father. But the very hairs of your head are all numbered. Fear ye not therefore, ye are of more value than many sparrows." In Luke 12:6 He says of the sparrows, "...not one of them is forgotten before God?" A falling tree makes a sound and is heard, if not by man then certain y by the One who made our ears (Ps. 94:7-9). God hears and knows all: falling sparrows, trees, hairs, and *all our thoughts, prayers, and our worship*.

One way to view the third question is to consider that under an electron microscope the head of a pin would seem larger than a football field. In that proportion lots of angels (of microscopic size) could dance there. That suggests that our senses and our perception of the spiritual and the natural, as between the readily observable and the microscopic, is not all there is to reality. Paul wrote "There are also celestial bodies and bodies terrestrial... "There is a natural body and... a spiritual body" (I Cor. 15:40, 44). He was describing the difference between our own natural bodies and our eternal incorruptible spiritual bodies. There is also a difference between the spiritual bodies of angels and the natural world which somehow allows them to move and interact with the natural; to even dance on the head of a pin (if they wanted to).

God does not merely inhabit *the praises* of His people as per Psalm 22:3. **He inhabits His people**. Spiritual reality and interactions with the natural are more complicated than the microscopic world. We occasionally catch a glimpse of the joy and singing in heaven (Lk. 15:7, Rev. 5:9, 14:3; 15:3). We can sometimes access it through worship. At times angels participate in our worship as well. I am sure they enjoy that more than dancing on a pin!

The exact mechanism whereby a room full of people can be joined by a multitude of angels may be unknown, but it can be perceived, with natural and spiritual senses (Lk. 2:9-14). I think angels enjoy our worship. The people do not get pushed aside by fluttering wings, nor are they stepped on by big angel feet even if all the seats and aisles are filled and the ceiling is low.

We all can fit together to worship the Incarnate Holy Lamb of God, who was slain to fully pay the penalty for the sins of all Mankind, who rose again, is seated at the right hand of the Father, and is worthy of all worship and praise (Phil. 5-11). That is what heaven is like. During times of prophetic worship, we sometimes get a foretaste of our eternal home. God is a Spirit. He is also a person (three persons) who can focus or localize and manifest His presence to be with us, to respond to us, and interact with us, even dance with us - *and He desires to do this.*

Knowing who God is, and having a personal relationship with Him by faith are both a prerequisite and a motivation for worshiping Him. Worship affirms who God is. The angels over the throne cry "...Holy, Holy, Holy, is the Lord of hosts: the whole earth is full of His glory" (Is. 6:3). To be worshipers of God in truth *our songs should declare who He is.* Worship should also proclaim the mystery of the Gospel (1 Timothy 3:16). Scriptural songs tell what He has done, and is doing, and will do. These are truths to which the Holy Spirit will bear witness (Jn. 15:26; 16:13) and that set the captive free (Jn. 8:32). Songs of worship that declare essential doctrines, such as who God is, and the good news of His atoning blood sacrifice for our redemption from sin and death into the family and Kingdom of our Lord Jesus Christ, lead toward **worship in Spirit and in Truth** (Jn. 4:23, 24).

Jesus said "If a man love me, he will keep my words: and my Father will love him, and **we** will come unto him, and make our abode with him." (John 14:23). Jesus said, "I will pray the Father, and he shall give you another Comforter, that he may abide with you for ever; Even the Spirit of truth; whom the world cannot receive, because it seeth him not, neither knoweth him: but ye know him; for he dwelleth with you, and shall be **in** you." (John 14:16-17). Are you feeling crowded thinking about being in the presence of the Three-in-One God and His Angels? I hope not. We are called to reach out with the gospel to bring in even more disciples into the family of God. There is plenty of room!

The skeptics point out hand clapping changes the galvanic skin response, effects the adrenal glands, and is used in hypnosis. Don't forget the existential moment, and a heightened psychological awareness, a vivid imagination, emotional instability, hallucinations, inebriation and mass hysteria. Then, consider those theologians who have decided that the things of the second chapter of Acts are not for now. But remember this too, **the tomb is empty**. Our God created us and desires to dwell with us and wants to reveal Himself to us. He wants to commune and have fellowship with His people.

Various natural aspects of worship are woven into this book, but are specifically considered in chapters VIII and XII to XIV. We live in both the Spiritual and the natural realm. How can we love God and each other as Christ loved us? (John 14:15; 15:12-13). "He must increase, but I must decrease" (John 3:30). Can this be a lifestyle and not just a momentary feeling? When we love another, for example a spouse or a child, our thoughts and actions can at times be with that person more than with ourselves. When faced with a crisis, in a family or a community, our focus can be more on the persons in need than on ourselves. "Me and my" becomes, "You, and yours." In worship, our thoughts and actions are redirected toward God, and away from ourselves. This happens all the more when God manifestly shows up in a release of the Spirit!

* * * * * * * *

Quench not the Spirit. Despise not prophesying. Prove all things; hold fast that which is good. Abstain from all appearance of evil. 1 Thessalonians 5:19-22.

I will pray with the spirit, and I will pray with the understanding also: I will sing with the spirit, and I will sing with the understanding also. Let all things be done decently and in order. 1 Corinthians 14: 15, 40.

Let the word of Christ dwell in you richly in all wisdom; **teaching and admonishing** one another in psalms and hymns and spiritual songs, singing with grace in your hearts to the Lord. Whatsoever you do in word or deed, do all in the name of the Lord Jesus, giving thanks to God and the Father by him. Colossians 3:16-17.
(Pause often to listen during worship.)

II - The Call
- How We Worship

The temple was in disrepair, the kingdom was in apostasy, and the prophets could only foresee destruction ahead. The portions of the worshipers had not been given them; therefore the musicians and the singers that did the work were fled every one to his field (Neh. 13:10). The High priest made this announcement, "The worshipers have left off the ministry to God in the temple and our whole nation suffers. We will therefore begin a screening process to recruit singers and musicians to do the work of the ministry so that our God will be pleased with us and our nation will no longer suffer." The notice was posted throughout the land. Many candidates came to the city to apply for this work.

All the important priests and wise judges sat behind tables near the entrance to the Holy place. There they could intensely interview the prospective worshipers who filed past them in long lines. At each point along the tables there were stacks of forms to be filled out, fees had to be paid, and questions answered. One special table, with an ornate and colorful cloth covering, was set up for those who had completed several years of studies of the sacred writings. Only the best educated and wealthiest candidates were directed to it. Off to one side was a gorgeously arrayed stage where the musicians and singers could audition. To help them get in the mood they were provided with elaborately decorated robes, almost as fine as priestly garments.

When God heard about it He decided to pay the place a visit too. He came to see if any of the people who wanted to be worshipers really would listen to His voice and commune with Him. He enjoyed fellowshipping with Adam, and Enoch, and Noah, and Abraham, and Isaac, and Jacob, and Moses, and Joshua, and Samuel, and all His many friends. In fact He desires to have a face-to-face relationship with all of His children. He sat Himself down, out of sight, on a box in a little room behind a curtain and tried to communicate with everyone who came through the line. He called out to each applicant, by name, and told them to move toward the opposite wall, away from the tables and the crowd; to move toward where He was sitting.

5

Someone asked about the weather, thinking it had thundered. A few fell down, rolling and crying out. "Show-offs," mumbled the judges. "We don't need that sort of thing around here." Some of the candidates began to insist that the whole thing was set up wrong; that the tables had to be moved to the opposite wall, in the direction the Lord was indicating for them privately. They even got into shouting and shoving matches over where to put the tables and where the priests should sit. Nobody moved toward God or to where he indicated.

Every now and then one or two would turn, nervously, hesitantly, and stare at the far wall with an inquisitive look on their face. When that happened one of the priests would shove more paper work in their direction and remind them that the job required the ability to get all the forms filled out right and on time. Nobody moved toward God.

So God moved. One of the angels thought He heard Him say to Himself as He left; "with Mo and Josh I had to wait 40 years, then after each generation I had to wait 40 years. No more, not again, not for 10 times 40 years."

* * * * * * * * * * * *

"Now in the fifteenth year of the reign of Tiberius Caesar, Pontius Pilate being governor of Judea, and Herod being tetrarch of Galilee, and his brother Philip being tetrarch of Ituraea, and of the region of Trachonitis, and Lysanias the tetrarch of Abilene, Annas and Caiphas being the high priests, the word of God came unto John the son of Zacharias in the wilderness." (Luke 3:1). Someone, somewhere, at sometime will listen to God.

The Oxford Dictionary of American English defines "spirit" as: the immaterial, intellectual, or moral part of man. A person's mind, soul, nature, or mood, liveliness, assertiveness, underlying meaning, or a disembodied soul. Finally, after #4, an elf or goblin, it mentions God, #5. This comes before the definition of spirit as: a distilled extract, alcohol.

Webster's Dictionary gives another definition first: a life-giving force, the active presence of God in human life, the third person of the trinity. Then it includes the other, natural uses, of the word. Those who define the words we think and communicate with may either undermine or support our approach to, and our understanding of God; they build bridges or barriers with dictionaries or with commentaries. Our worship is communion with the living creator God, by and because of the life-giving active presence of God in our lives. We worship the risen living Son of the living God and the living Holy Spirit.
This is **Worship in Spirit and in Truth.**

III - The Reward - Why We Worship

"But without faith it is impossible to please him; for he that cometh to God must believe that he is, and that he is a **rewarder** of them that diligently seek him." (Hebrews 11:6). Believe and diligently seek are our part, and that only by the enabling grace of God. What about the reward? That is His part. What is the outcome or reward of worship?

When entering the presence of God there is an experience of joy and peace, "good" feelings. There may be an impartation of strength or health. Many people experience deliverance from the chains that bind them; both the psychological kind, such as anxiety, fear, or worry, and the biological kind, such as addictions to alcohol, tobacco, or other substances (Isaiah. 10:27). There is also a sense of unity and purpose with other worshipers involved. The worship may be an involvement with prayerful petitions. It might be a spiritual warfare which effects those participating, or which helps other people at some other location or time. It may be a preparation for something soon to take place.

This is not the reward. The coin of the realm, that which is most valuable of the Kingdom of God, is God Himself. "And ye shall seek me, and find me, when ye shall search for me with all your heart." (Jer. 29:13). "I love them that love me; and those that seek me early will find me." "That I may cause those that love me to inherit substance and I will fill their treasures." (Prov. 8:17, 21; 1 Cor. 1:30, Col. 2:3). "He that hath my commandments, and keepeth them, he it is that loveth me, and he that loveth me shall be loved of my Father, and I will love him, and **will manifest** myself to him" (Jn. 14:21).

That substance we partake of in worship, the greatest treasure of all, is God Himself. True, we love Him because He first loved us and gave Himself for us, but worship is more than a reminder of a past blessing. It is a present relationship. God still delights to manifestly visit and commune with those who delight to be His people! Corporate or private worship is one way we enjoy His presence and he enjoys us as individuals. Where two or more gather in his name he is there in their midst (Matt. 18:20). When the desire of our hearts is to be with him, he will meet with us (Psalm 37:34).

When we are born again we get a down payment (II Cor. 2:22), a taste (Ps. 34:8). The taste of God both satisfies and ruins us for anything else. Only the substance of God Himself can satisfy. As we worship, exalt, and glorify our Lord

Jesus Christ, acknowledging His presence and rightful place, with a focus and purpose of communion and fellowship with God, we become more like him and like him more. The reward of worship, regardless of what else transpires (and much does), is God Himself. Christ in you, the hope of glory (Col. 1:27).

We begin an active relationship with God when we are saved, born again, and filled with the Holy Spirit. Just as with natural life, we know we are alive in the Spirit when we begin to be hungry for the Word of God (I Peter 2:2), The Bible teaches that we are *becoming sons of God*, (Jn. 1:12), *growing* into the fullness of the stature and image of Jesus Christ, (Eph. 4:13). As we behold His image we are *being changed* from glory to glory by the Spirit of the Lord (II Cor 3:18). All living things need nourishment, they must feed and grow.

The best gifts, the best rewards, are those that are needed and most appropriate. When we are convicted of sin, and repent, and ask Jesus to save us, we are born again. Being born again means we become a spiritual baby. Alive yes, but a newborn. "As newborn babes, desire the sincere milk of the word, that ye may grow thereby." (I Peter 2:2). Everyone who is saved by faith in Christ has begun a relationship with God and can anticipate eternity in heaven with God, but we should desire to see that relationship grow along the way.

* * * * * * * *

What are **eternal rewards**? In our natural life, a five year old would be thrilled to receive a tricycle as a gift or reward. A fifteen year old teenager might be happy to receive a driver education course. A twenty-five year old would likely delight to receive a new car. If their gifts were reversed, or they all got only the same gift or reward, they would not be satisfied or even able to use it. Relationships also change as we grow; from acquaintance, to friend, to spouse. Our rewards in heaven are also like this. Christians will receive what are the most appropriate rewards (Rev. 22:12). These will be the result of our maturity in Christ reached during our lifetime of walking with him. If we are faithful with what we receive in this life we will hear "well done, good and faithful servant," and receive appropriate rewards (Matt. 25:15-30).

Everyone in heaven will be with God and will be satisfied. No one will be bored in eternity. Now, in this lifetime, is the time when I must ask myself the question, "in heaven will I be more like a five year old child enjoying a tricycle, or more like a thirty-three year old adult nailed to a cross?" We each have that choice to make with our life.

8

IV - Revivals - Who Is Involved

Revivals in New York City clogged churches, emptied bars, and brought a city to its knees in prayer and repentance. In upstate New York the preaching of Charles Finney closed factories, opened churches and changed hearts. Throughout the history of our country, as with the Church world-wide since the Book of Acts, revivals are major events awakening and renewing faith and growing the family of God.

Men and women of faith carried out the great commission in the United States, at times leading to a Great Awakening. In the early 18th century, the evangelist called Johnny Appleseed planted more than natural fruit trees. Shubal Stearns founded a church at Sandy Creek, North Carolina which spread to give birth to almost a thousand frontier churches that became the Southern Baptist Convention. These were forerunners of Billy Sunday and Billy Graham of the 20th century to mention two of many. At the Cane Ridge revival in Kentucky, or the Azuza Street mission in Los Angeles, or North Battleford, Saskatchewan, or Detroit, Michigan, or to prayer groups in Indiana, or Kansas, revival has flowed like cool water to a parched earth, or like a roaring fire. In Seattle, Brownsville, or Redding, in Wales, England, Europe, or China, India, Africa, Asia, Australia, New Zealand, and from Buenos Aires to Toronto, and to new and unknown places, wherever hearts hunger for eternal reality from God there has and there will be revival.

In whatever group, and whatever they call themselves, or however they label the experience of the manifest presence of God, be they Shakers, or Quakers, Anglicans, or Episcopalians, Methodists, or Baptists, Moravians, Presbyterians, or Brethren, Lutherans, Mennonites, Reformed, or Nazarenes, Church of God, Church of Christ, Assembly of God, Four Square, Christian and Missionary Alliance, Latter Rain, Full Gospel, or Charismatic, or Catholic, (to name a few), there has been revival and renewal from Heaven. God is involved with His creation. He is building His Church and preparing His Bride.

These groups were either begun by or greatly influenced by revival, renewal, as well as by times of refreshing (Acts 3:19). For some it manifested as a quickening of the Word of God. For others as a convicting of sin and a longing for holiness. Others were moved to reconciliation or outreach to the community. Some have reached out to the whole world, or engaged in all of the above and more.

Souls were saved and some were overwhelmed with the power of God, such as by manifestations or gifts of the Holy Spirit, such as tongues, prophecy, healing or miracles as the Apostle Paul mentioned in I Cor. 12:8-10. This includes behavior that resembles drunkenness as described in Acts 2:13. In addition, all of these groups were moved upon to worship God. New songs are one of the earmarks of revival, renewal, refreshing, and Spiritual awakening.

Missionaries carry a Bible and a hymnal to the field. The Holy Ghost comes with a song of praise and worship to our God. This Amazing Grace may begin in the heart of one saved sinner and set fire to a community, or begin a blaze that travels around the nation, the continent, and the world.

It is strange to see how this has happened to so many people and different groups and then each one thinks that they are the only ones God moves upon in this way. A touch from heaven is taken to be justification or confirmation of whatever it is that happens to be going on at the time for that individual or group. Then we, like Peter on the Mount of Transfiguration, build a tabernacle or a monument to our experience to permanently enshrine it. Along with this we create "spiritual rules" as to why and how the Holy Spirit is moving, what God is doing it for, and what techniques or means are required to maintain or recreate the experience of revival. Since the birth of the Church each revival seems to lead to pronouncements that "this is the last big one, get with it," and "these are the things you must do to move with God." Tell that to the first church at Jerusalem.

One reason for this is that there is usually some kind of battle and a price to pay that makes the revival dear to participants and engenders possessiveness toward it. It is not just the unsaved who resist. There is often opposition from within the church which brings a sense of betrayal by one's own family. This hurts much worse than being hurt by a stranger. God manifests and ministers to those who respond to His moving, but one sad result of revival may be a hurt and hardness which remain for years even despite efforts toward repentance and healing hearts.

Singing in tongues, prophesying, raising hands, or dancing in the Spirit are examples of Biblical forms of worship. When a church government says, "stop or leave," a split occurs. The many scriptures which exhort to dance, prophesy, clap or raise your hands are used as defense, but to no avail. The scripture gets ignored or misinterpreted and used to suit one side or another. The focus on correct public worship is so strong it leads to misuse of the Bible.

Pride, prestige, and position are challenged. Sides are drawn, black and white, right and wrong. The cry becomes, "God is with us, not you." The Holy Spirit bears witness to certain things and a new movement is born. Sadly, many hard feelings and excesses come along with worship.

One example is the song "If you want joy," you must get it by clapping, jumping, and dancing. It may seem childish, but it can still be fun and good for exercise. On the other hand, exhorting people to dance by singing "I shall yet be more vile" from II Sam. 6:22, infers that dancing as part of worship is vile and it ignores the weightier issues of that scripture.

The people of the Middle East and Europe dance in worship more than we do. Americans are less comfortable with dancing than are people from Middle Eastern cultures. That is no reason to pervert the scripture. In many countries people still greet each other with a kiss. Imagine exhorting this practice, which Paul mentions, by using a scripture that showed a disciple doing it: Judas kissed Jesus, and then ignoring the main events of that story. God forbid! When hearts grow cold or weary there are better scriptures than II Sam. 6:22 to use to encourage an enthusiastic worship, or to use to guard against a judgmental attitude about worship.

At least since Matthew Henry's commentary on the Bible the story of David's victory celebration (II Sam. 6:15-23) has been interpreted this way. He interpreted the story as an example of a conflict between the religious and the irreligious. In our day, quiet, reserved, mainline denominations use this passage to encourage people to sing the old hymns with more force and vigor. It is not just Pentecostal or Charismatic enthusiasm that is exhorted this way. There are many scriptures which exhort us to love the Lord our God with all our strength; with body, soul, and spirit, and not to despise the moving of the spirit. Jews will often rock back and forth and gyrate their bodies while praying in order to fulfill Deut. 6:5. Jesus goes so far as to say He will vomit out of His mouth those who are only lukewarm toward Him (Rev. 3:16). Worship is not always a quiet activity.

Worship and moving with the fire of the Holy Spirit are vital. However, using the story of David and Michal for the purpose of exhorting dancing in worship is calling good evil, and evil good. It overshadows and ignores the story and important messages those scriptures teach.

Consider what happened. Michal's family was killed. She is then taken from her husband, for the second time, contrary to law (II Sam. 3:13-16, Deut. 24:1-4). Her life and all her joy has been destroyed because of the conflict between David and Saul.

David abandoned her. He left her to face her father Saul who had earlier tried to kill her brother Jonathan because he disobeyed him by eating a little honey. In order to save her life she tells her father that David had threatened to kill her if she did not let him go. Years later David takes her from her new home. She sees him rejoicing and celebrating his victory with exuberant dancing. She hates him, even despises him, and mocks his behavior when they meet. Therefore they have no relationship and she has no children.

Teaching that this was due to her mocking his dancing is to condone kidnaping and divorce and ignore the politics of the event. It obscures right from wrong. The story has little to do with dancing or being religious or irreligious, nor is it for or against enthusiastic worship of God. This is a sad, tragic story.

Jesus rebuked the scribes and Pharisees for being more concerned with their form of worship than with the "...weightier matters of the law, judgment, mercy and faith..." (Matt. 23:23). Many scholars acknowledge, "...a weightier cause than David's dancing" for the quarrel between David and Michal. David most likely demanded the return of his divorced and remarried former wife because he wanted to limit competition and add justification to his claim to the throne. He was not relying solely on God's election (see The Interpreter's Bible, Vol. II, pages 1059 & 1082, Abingdon Press, NY, 1953). And as for being more vile, David later offered human sacrifice, also against God's law. He ordered the killing of seven more of Michal's family! (II Sam. 21:1-11). Should these things be ignored in order to exhort dancing as part of our more lively worship?

The behavior of David and Michal is all too familiar to pastors and church counselors. Too many marriages in our country end in divorce. In 2016, almost 30% of the children in America grow up in single parent homes. How vile people can get is seen most vividly when love turns to hate. This is an important Bible story to explore; a "weightier matter." It should not get overshadowed by dancing or by any other type or expression of enthusiastic worship.

The story is rarely told, but it does not end there. David had many faults. Adultery and murder are the most well known. When his daughter was raped he did nothing, he again ignored God's law. On his death bed David's heart was full of vengeance, not mercy and forgiveness.

The sweet psalmist of Israel as a King, Prophet, and Priest is a type of Jesus. As a man, David is an example of God's election and forgiveness. However, God's love moves beyond forgiveness. He also changes lives. We see a conflict between Jesus and another Saul in the book of Acts. God's love transforms that Saul into the Apostle Paul. This Jesus, of whom David was but a shadowy type, rather than dancing, writhes on a cross between heaven and earth at the end of the old and the bringing in of a new kingdom.

When the divorced wife of Jesus, remarried to the carnal and a slave to sin, mocks and spits on Him, even beats and crucifies Him, He loves her to redemption. He does not flee from her to protect Himself. He lays down His life for her. After His resurrection He causes her to be fruitful. There is reconciliation in this story. That is something to dance, shout, sing, and celebrate about!

Of course there is more than one way to tell and apply a Bible story. For example, the parable of the seeds and the sower may be interpreted either to suggest degrees of spiritual fruitfulness: 30%, 60%, or 100%, or as a description of different types of trees: grapefruit, apple, or cherry, which produce different amounts of fruit, but all at 100% of their intended capacity. Teaching either one will not corrupt the scripture. Each view adds something. However, just as his defining "prophesying" to mean "preaching," is wrong and defrauds the church of the Holy Spirit's gift of prophecy, Matthew Henry's use of the conflict between David and Michal to contrast proper religion and disrespect for zealousness does disservice to the church. It is unfortunate that during the excitement of a genuine move of the Holy Spirit we sometimes misinterpret the moment or the Bible.

The Holy Spirit may bear witness to dancing with all our might before the Lord. This is a truth about worship found in scripture. Much happens in the spiritual realm during and because of this. Those who reject this, who fail to respond to this leading of the Holy Spirit, may become spiritually barren, or God may have something else for them. However, that is not the point of the David and Michal story. God is preparing a glorious church for Himself, one without spot or wrinkle - not a vile one! **Dance in Spirit and in Truth.**

* * * * * * * *

13

A Note About *Solos*

Some say the greatest solo was when God sang the universe into existence – in the key of C (John 1:3).

The Shema declares God is One (Deut. 6:4). Christianity is monotheistic too (Mark 12:29). We worship the Three-in-One, the Father, Son, and Holy Spirit.

The five Solos of the Reformation, as themes or slogans for preaching and singing, should not be *deified* since they are not solos. Luther is reported as having said "salvation is by faith alone, but faith is never alone" (*refer* to James 2:26).

We are saved by faith in Christ alone, but when Jesus the Great R*eviver* saves us, both Jesus and the Father live in us (John 14:23). This is by grace alone, so let us not resist, but boldly approach, fully receive, and bear good fruit (Heb. 3:14-15, 4:7 & 16; II Cor. 6:1).

Scripture alone, the highest *level* of doctrinal authority, is not alone in that *top spot.* A *tenet* of scripture is, how shall anyone hear without a sent preacher (Rom. 10:14-15).

All we are and do is for the glory of God alone, but Jesus wants us to see His glory (John 17:24; II Cor.3:18).

In Lone Ranger *sagas* he's despised by the greedy,
so he tries to disguise his real name.
His vow, when *reviled, "deliver* the needy,
and though *evil live* on ride away with no fame."
Yet each *mom and pop* with an *s.o.s.* shows,
this long-ago legend speaks loud.
Like the real Lamb who died for our sin then arose,
he knows each as a friend, not a crowd.

V - Preparation for Individual and Group Worship

We love Him because He first loved us (1 John 4:19).

Come unto me all ye who labour and are heavy laden and I will give you rest. Take my yoke upon you and learn of me, for I am meek and lowly in heart, and you will find rest unto your souls (Matthew 11:28-30, KJV). Coming to Jesus leads to becoming a worshiper.

Present your bodies as a living sacrifice, holy and acceptable to God, which is your spiritual worship. Do not be conformed to this world, but be transformed by the renewing of your minds. (Romans12:1-2, NRSV)

Seek the LORD while he may be found, call upon him while he is near (Isaiah 55:6). When you said, seek my face; my heart said to you, "Your face, Lord, will I seek" (Psalm 27:8). You shall find me when you search for me with all your heart (Jeremiah 29:13).

One thing have I desired of the Lord, that will I seek after; that I may dwell in the house of the Lord all the days of my life, to behold the beauty of the Lord, (Psalm 27:4). Desire, seek, and behold the living God.

Wait on the Lord (Psalm 27:14). Where two or three are gathered together in my name, there am I in their midst (Matthew 18:20). Wait on, recognize and worship God.

Be still and know that I am God (Psalm 46:10). Be quick to hear, slow to speak (James 1:19). Listen! Worship is a two way conversation, a dialogue, not just singing at the Lord. My house shall be called an house of prayer for all people (Isaiah 56:7). Listen!

Look to Jesus. He is true, honest, just, pure, lovely, of good report, virtue, and praiseworthy (Philippians 4:8). I will meditate on your precepts (Psalm 119:15).

Begin worship by worshiping. Enter into his gates with thanksgiving and into his courts with praise. Be thankful unto him, and bless his Holy name (Psalm 100:4).

Appropriate Attire for Worship
What to Wear and How to Dress

Create in me a clean heart, O God; and renew a right spirit within me. The sacrifice of God is a broken spirit. He wilt not despise a contrite heart (Psalm 51:10–17).

Adorn yourselves in respectable apparel with modesty and self-control (I Timothy 2:9).

I will rejoice in the Lord, my soul shall be joyful in my God. He clothed me with a garment of salvation, He covered me with a robe of righteousness (Isaiah 61:10).

Put on a garment of praise (Isaiah. 61:3). Put on mercy, kindness, humility, meekness, longsuffering; bearing with one another, and forgiving one another. If anyone has a complaint against another; even as Christ forgave you, so you also do. But above all, put on love, which is the bond of perfection (Colossians 3:12-14).

Be clothed with humility (1 Peter 5:5). Be reconciled to your brother, then come and offer your gift (Matthew. 5:24).

Put on the whole armor of God, girding your loins with truth and having on the breastplate of righteousness and your feet shod with the preparation of the gospel of peace. Above all, take the shield of faith wherewith you are able to quench all the fiery darts of the wicked one. Pray always with prayer and supplication in the Spirit for all saints. Take the helmet of salvation, and the sword of the Spirit–the word of God (Eph. 6:11-17).

Choose you this day whom you will serve. As for me and my house, we will serve the Lord (Joshua. 24:15). Commit to being a worshiper of the Lord Jesus Christ.

VI - Making Contact - A Process

The Holy Spirit will point toward Jesus and testify to the truth. Jesus will worship the Father in the midst of the congregation (Heb. 2:12). The angels around the throne are always worshiping. From time to time during the history of the church, Adam's race has been allowed to experience and join in this glorious communion. Some claim it is just a preview, not to be the standard for now, merely a foretaste of heavenly worship.

Imagine reciting a beautiful love sonnet to your spouse. He or she is standing right there next to you. You speak well, in a clear, firm, loud voice, getting the words right, articulating, enunciating and emoting perfectly. You never make eye contact, never reach out and touch, embrace, or even hold your beloved's hand. When it is over, you sit down and get on with whatever other business is at hand. What is wrong with this picture?

Now do the same thing every week in church to the Lord Jesus Christ, our heavenly bridegroom. "...I would thou wert cold or hot... Behold, I stand at the door and knock..." (Rev. 3:15-16, 20). If this seems to suggest some measure of "emotionalism," consider the sonnet. Are love, thanksgiving, or the affirmation of Emmanuel - God with us, emotional, passionate statements? Not everyone connects with God through worship, - but for those who do....

The worship begins, hesitantly, listening more than singing, straining the senses for an updraft, a touch of, or the fragrance of the Lord. Then, it seems as though the heavens open and the physical walls and ceiling become porous to let Eternity in. The worship flows, it takes on direction and meaning. Just like prayer it may be confession, intercession, petition, thanksgiving, or praise and adoration or something else.

The songs may take on a responsiveness: perhaps the voice of the bridegroom, followed by the voice of the bride. Then prophetic worship may occur, originating from the Son, the Holy Spirit, or the Father. As the manifest presence of God is recognized the sense of purpose may intensify.

Individual voices may be used or sections of a congregation may be played like the instruments in some heavenly orchestra or choir. Wave after wave of heavenly anointing flows through the worship. The presence of God and even a supernatural fragrance of incense, perfumes, perhaps even grape wine, permeates the meeting. There is a sense, as spoken by the two on the road to Emmaus, "Did not our hearts burn within us when he spoke." This may last minutes or hours. The singing may be noteworthy, or perhaps ministry is taking place with healings, or words of prophecy entering directly into hearts, perhaps with no one but God speaking directly to individuals. This is **worship in Spirit and in Truth**.

Conducting such a symphony can be heady stuff. Talk about feeling ten feet tall! There may be an intense desire to fall on your knees, or on your face! (II Chron. 5:13-14, Is. 6:1-7, Rev. 1:17). The worship leader may receive a word in advance that this is going to take place or it could come as a surprise. It may flow through his or her being and ignite the congregation. It could originate from some other focal point or be more of a general upsurge. It may arise out of another's prayerful intercession or seem to be just like the anointing for any other prophetic ministry. The worship leader may receive insight into individuals and what God is doing, or going to do in their lives. Then the decision has to be made as to whether the unction and leading is there to do personal and/or public ministry or not.

The leader may try to move the congregation toward some point or he or she may have to step out of the way. There may be a need to make sure others do not get in the way. The Holy Spirit is gentle, and God often speaks in a still small voice. It takes great grace, and a sensitivity to the moving of God, to flow with this exalted worship, and to *not* try to steer it, or control and dominate it with rhythm, or with a natural enthusiasm or goal. Such power can be intoxicating, and such glory may spoil you for any other natural activity, such as leading a sing-along, or the making of even the most beautiful earthly music. **Worship in Spirit and in Truth** will definitely change all who enter these Heavenly realms!

VII - The Lord's Minstrels

Minstrels, in olden days, were privileged with safe passage between warring feudal estates. When minstrels visited a castle, it meant a chance to hear the latest news from far away places and to listen to some fairly good, or at least different, music. They would be welcomed, fed, housed, and honored, until their news and songs were used up. Then they'd move on to the next isolated oasis. Radio, TV and the Internet have not completely replaced this.

Today, for the Lord's minstrels, troubadours, or balladeers, doors to any group or denomination are often open to music and stories, and to clowns and puppeteers. Churches that would never allow an outsider access to their pulpit to preach or teach will welcome, with little questioning or referral, the ministry of the minstrel. As long as the Gospel is simple, the songs scriptural, the stories directed toward faith in Jesus, and controversy is avoided, the doors for visiting ministry may open. Change is refreshing and welcomed from time to time.

The best time is for Sunday or mid-week evening services but sometimes the main Sunday morning gathering is open too. BTW, A simple scriptural Gospel message directed at faith in Jesus Christ and avoiding controversy is also the way to come into an anointing from God. To find God's unction and presence, go where He goes, then, give yourself away. Doors will often open at: nursing homes, hospitals, hospices, prisons, youth homes, group homes for the cognitively impaired, or to any other needy group that can not pay you (Is. 61:1-3).

Music is part of many church structures, like pews or a pulpit. Most people in the congregation have focused all week on earning a living in a secular world. They come to church to receive something; to be strengthened and refreshed. When pressed as to what song is in their hearts the only response may be a child's Bible song memorized years earlier at camp, or the latest jingle from the radio they listened to driving to church. There may be no song in their heart. They need yours. Give it away. "Comfort ye my people." More comfort and strength is available by entering into worship, but there is a price to pay for that. Not everyone has that ministry or can receive it (I Cor. 12: 14, 29, 30).

The role and life of worship leaders, is to set themselves on fire by entering deeply into intimate communion with the Lord. That fire is God's manifest presence that invites and moves the congregation to worship. This is totally unlike cheer leading, pumping up, calisthenics, sing-alongs, or theatrics. Rhythm, emotion, personality, and electronics all get used to manipulate people to sing. The Holy Spirit of God is altogether different than our motivational techniques. He leads **worship in Spirit and in Truth.**

If you wanted to get your prayers answered, or to become a prayer warrior, there are certain ones to go to in church to learn from. Something about the way they pray gives the sense that God is right there with them, perhaps with a hand on their shoulder listening. It is no secret really. They are gifted to live a life of prayer that invites the presence of the Lord to be with them. How to be a worshiper or worship leader is no secret. Spend your life at it.

A musician lives a life of practice. Many times people ask to be prayed for to be able to play a musical instrument. The prayer goes like this, "Lord please give my (brother or sister) the patience to repeat physically demanding movements endlessly for hours, days, weeks, months and years. Allow them the tolerance to experience failure thousands of times more than they experience success. Grant them the joy that comes from spending time alone; to decline social activities in order to concentrate on their instrument. Permit them to be the center of attention for a few minutes every once and awhile, without getting puffed up, then to be ignored while people who cultivate other things in their life, have a life. Make the association of their identity with an inanimate wood or metal object a fulfilling emotional experience. And Lord, if you should permit them to have no family, or gainful employment, in order to provide music in the church, for 5, 6, 7, or more services and special occasions a week, as a volunteer without pay, please turn their poverty and loneliness into joy, or provide a part-time job that doesn't interfere with the church schedule. Amen."

If the person asking for prayer is not restrained they will usually be gone before this prayer is finished. A dentist or a mechanic should be paid for their labor, but to some, music is a "free gift." In 2014, when the average, teaching pastor received $45,000 per year, a worship leader or coordinator, if any compensation is given, might have earned $23,000.

When people ask for prayer to play an instrument, so they can worship God, the response is different. **Put down the instrument**, lift up your hands and voice, and worship the Lord. Prayer warriors pray. Worshipers worship. They spend **time,** alone and with others, worshiping. That and God's grace is all it takes, and that is God's grace. Seek the Lord, is how to get to be a worshiper; don't stop, is how to stay one. If concentration is on the instrument being learned, or the words being sung, how can our heart and attention be focused on God?

In his book "The Pursuit of God," A. W. Tozer wrote a prayer which is a request to be a worshiper. "I want to want thee, I long to be filled with longing, I thirst to be made more thirsty, that I may know Thee oh God." Ask God to enlarge your desire and capacity to commune with Him, then spend time with Him, be in His presence, and worship Him.

* * * * * * * *

Philippians. 2:5-11 Let this mind be in you, which was also in Christ Jesus: Who, being in the form of God, thought it not robbery to be equal with God: But made himself of no reputation, and took upon him the form of a servant, and was made in the likeness of men: And being found in fashion as a man, he humbled himself, and became obedient unto death, even the death of the cross. Wherefore God also hath highly exalted him, and given him a name which is above every name: That at the name of Jesus every knee should bow, of things in heaven, and things in earth, and things under the earth; And that every tongue should confess that Jesus Christ is Lord, to the glory of God the Father.

* * * * * * * *

Everything we have, every breath we take is a gift from God (Col. 1:16). God is the Creator and giver of everything (Eph. 3:9). We must avoid worshiping the creation more than the Creator (Ro. 1:25). We can want from Him what He wants to give us and we can desire most what He most wants to give us. He creates and gives us the desire of our hearts (Psalm 37:4).

* * * * * * * *

"Only one life, t'will soon be past,
 only what's done for Christ will last."   (C.T. Studd).

* * * * * * *

We worship a Holy God.

Holy,: Divine, Deity, sacred, dedicated, sanctified, set-apart, consecrated to the service of God,

Leviticus 11: 44, 20:7, [44]For I *am* the LORD your God: ye shall therefore sanctify yourselves, and ye shall **be holy**; for I *am* holy: [7]Sanctify yourselves therefore, and **be ye holy**: for I *am* the LORD your God.

Isaiah 6:3, [3]: . . "**Holy, holy, holy** is the LORD of hosts; the whole earth is full of his glory!"

Psalm 99:9, Exalt the LORD our God, and worship at his holy mountain; for **the LORD our God is holy**!

II Corinthians 7:1, [1]Having therefore these promises, dearly beloved, let us cleanse ourselves from all filthiness of the flesh and spirit, **perfecting holiness** in the fear of God.

Hebrews 12:14, [14]Follow peace with all men and **holiness**, without which no man shall see the Lord:

1 Peter 1:15-16 [15]But as he which hath called you is **holy**, so be ye **holy** in all manner of conversation; [16]Because it is written, Be ye **holy**; for I am **holy.**

Revelation 4:8 . . . **Holy, holy, holy**, Lord God Almighty, which was, and is, and is to come.

VIII - Liberty In The Lord (II Cor. 3:17)

The story is told of an oriental emperor who, one day, took a walk in the forest. He heard the most beautiful music coming from a tree above his head. He visited that spot each day at the same time to listen to the beautiful music that somehow seemed to soothe his soul from all the cares and worries of the empire. He sent his wise men to the forest to find out where the music was coming from. He was informed. "It is the mockingbird."

The very next day he went out to his favorite spot and after listening to the mockingbird sing called out to it, "Oh beautiful mockingbird, if you will come to the castle with me, and sing for me I will take care of you, and give you all your heart's desire in food and riches beyond your wildest dreams." "The forest provides for all my needs," replied the mockingbird. "I have no need for anything more." "But you will be famous, everyone will hear you," the emperor said. "The Creator of all hears me now," answered the little bird, "who else is more important than that?" The emperor pleaded and at last the mockingbird said, "for your sake I will come."

The emperor's craftsmen built a beautiful, ornate, golden, cage for the mockingbird who would sing for the emperor when he was burdened or tired out from ruling the vast country. Sometimes he would be called upon to perform for visitors at fancy parties or elaborate state dinners, which he did without complaint or demand for anything for himself. No one seemed to notice that in captivity his feathers were losing their color or that his voice was not as sweet as it once was.

One day the emperor's wise men came to him with a surprise. They had built a little mechanical singing bird! They wound it up and it made the most delightful and varied music. It had feathers of pure gold and shone in the sunlight. They had placed jewels all around it which reflected even the candle light at night. Everyone, including the emperor, was impressed by the new toy.

Someone suggested it sounded better than the old mockingbird. Another music critic proposed a competition between the two to determine which one was the better singer, the real mockingbird or the mechanical one. It was really no contest. Everyone could see how inferior the real bird was. The machine won the contest. They put the golden mechanical bird into the golden cage and the real mockingbird flew back to the forest in disgrace.

Several years later, after an especially hard battle, the emperor was sick. All his physicians could not heal him for he was wounded in soul and in body. The mechanical bird sounded just like a machine to him, which of course it was, and it gave him no comfort. As he lay on his bed near death he sighed and said "if only I could hear one sweet song from the real mockingbird again, I am sure that music would restore me."

His prayer reached the little mockingbird in the whisper of the wind. He flew as fast as he could back to the castle and the window of the emperor. There, after catching his breath, he began to sing. The emperor sat up, then arose. A smile came to his face where before only gloom had been. "Is that you my little friend?" he called out. "Won't you please come back? I will build you a finer house. That awful machine will never again take your place."

"If you put me in a cage, no matter how fine it is, I will die. My song comes from the Spirit of the Creator and cannot be imprisoned anymore than you can chain the wind. But you are welcome to come to the forest to listen any time you wish and I will come here to sing for you from time to time," replied the mockingbird. Then he flew back to the forest.

* * * * * * * * * * *

A mechanical structure always becomes a problem. It is often viewed as necessary and it can help. We live first in the natural then in the spiritual (I Cor. 15:46). The difficulty is that the flesh lusteth against the spirit and the spirit against the flesh (Gal. 5:16-26). That is the greater problem which grows all the more as our tools and toys become more powerful This warfare is especially fierce in regard to individual and cooperate worship.

Music is one of God's gifts to man. What we make of it is our gift to Him. Submitted to Him it may become a vehicle for a depth of intimacy with God. He may use it to bless others. By itself, or even after being touched by God, it may be captured, diverted, and used for other purposes.

* * * * * * * * * * *

God instituted worship and He hates idolatry. He built a beautiful garden temple and put an image in it where He went to fellowship. In the cool of the day He communed and fellowshipped with the idol (an image of God) He had made and it reflected His image. In order to more clearly reflect His glory He cut the strings and gave us life and free choice. We used those gifts to pretend we are like a god, to create our own idols, and worship reflections of ourselves, rather than be a reflection and dwelling place of our Creator. Clearly reflecting God's image, as refined gold, or as a well polished mirror, is **worship in Spirit and in Truth.**

24

IX - Minstrel Nightmares

Our God is truly the God who communicates with His people. He is always in communion with His people. "The Word was made flesh and dwelt among us...." Worship is communion with God. "...not of the letter, but of the spirit: for the letter killeth, but the spirit bringeth life." (II Cor. 3:6). It should not seem a strange thing that God walks and talks and is involved with us today.

The anointing of God is attractive but those who are not familiar with it may think they are being attracted to the music or the person. "You must be anointed, you play so well," and "I'm in love with that worship leader," are not uncommon reactions. When the music or the person are uncommonly attractive, in the natural, they may tend to overshadow that still small voice of God speaking through them, or they may overwhelm an immature Christian's power of discernment. Music with a strong beat will do this. Rhythm may be a means to focus attention but it can easily dominate. What happens is people look to the music, or to the figure in front "on stage," or to the words in a book, or on a wall, into the face of electricity, instead of into the face of God.

Anointed worship is a prophetic activity. It requires a relationship with God through Jesus Christ of course. It also requires a life of holiness, being separated unto God, and *the sensitivity to respond to the moving of the Holy Spirit*.

Sometimes the expectation exists that worship should always be prophetic. The claim may be made that worship is always led by the Holy Spirit because the truth is always anointed. Songs with the Gospel and the Holy Word are a good start, but worship is not always prophetic and you can wear people out trying to get there. Stop and rest. Do not beat the sheep. Do not keep singing to try to move people into spiritual worship. And being loud is not the same as being spiritual. The moving of the Spirit of God cannot be forced and the spirit of the prophets is subject to the prophets. They can participate in formal, ritual worship and be a blessing, but they cannot survive for long that way.

Some worship teams meet during the week to practice songs. They may also set that time apart for prayer and prophetic worship among themselves. During the regular services they have to perform to meet the needs of the structure and time allowed.

When people first experience the prophetic worship meeting of a music ministry team they may insist it be opened up to everyone. Pretty soon there will be two churches under one roof; a worshiping church and a sing-along church. Then, rather than offend the more numerous members, the worshiping church may be suppressed. Prophetic worship can be shouted down and the worship leader easily replaced. Differences in styles or worship music may be cited as causing divisions in church, but conflict between flesh and Spirit, even with the same music is what leads to splits. Not everyone can perceive, or appreciate, or participate in prophetic worship.

This happens to intercessory prayer meetings that rise to the prophetic too. This is based on the false beliefs that the living and spiritual is inferior to, and can be submitted to the mechanical, or that everyone in a church can and should participate in all types of ministry to create a sense of unity. It may also happen due to the envy of those experiencing the obvious manifestation and favor of God. Cain and Abel, Saul and David are prominent examples.

Worship and praise get used for purposes other than communion with God. A leader suggested getting a Rock & Roll band saved to use them for worship services as a way to attract people and build a larger congregation. If a plumber's (free) service is needed, flatter him, place him in front of the congregation to preach or lead worship. It may be necessary to apologize for the *good* quality of a music ministry in order not to scare away the timid or offend the proud. There is a need to placate envy and jealousy. The worship leader may be informed after each service if the offering, which after all, comes after the worship, not after the preaching, is up or down. If it is down and his anointing or talent does not raise enough money. heads will roll. Music, *called* worship, is used for many natural purposes (see chapter XIII on the uses of music).

The seductive call of the "big time" is another minstrel nightmare. The fall of Lucifer is credited to his pride at being God's worship leader and wanting the glory for himself. The temptations; money and sex, plague those who succumb to pride and lust.

In that bleak pit individuals, families, and even churches are ruined. It destroys the "star," the "groupy," and even the "managers." Some churches wanted to raise money so they signed up a top name singer, rented a huge stadium, then went into shock when instead of making money they lost a bundle. They had not noticed that the words of their beautiful celebrity's latest secular hit were popular, but contrary to sound Christian doctrine. The glamour and riches of the spotlight blind many people and may overshadow Spirit and Truth.

In old testament times only a few specialists were chosen for the task of praising the Lord with instruments and singing (I Chr. 25:7). This they did day and night without concern for other things (I Chr. 9:33). Today there is confusion between worship, showmanship, and the glitz of stardom. In some places, worship is a concert. For others, there is a striving for laity participation and equality of function. Simple repetitive lines devoid of Biblical substance is required by claims that anything more complex is too difficult for "the people." This reaching for the lowest common denominator occurs when secular style entertainment influences worship.

"But we have this treasure in earthen vessels" (II Cor. 4:7). "If we confess our sins, he is faithful and just to forgive us our sins, and to cleanse us from all unrighteousness. If we say that we have not sinned we make him a liar".
(I Jn. 1: 9-10).

* * * * * * * *

A conference on worship was held with over 2,000 attending. In the back rooms and in secret wealthy leaders of large churches, denominations, and the Music Industrial Complex divided up the American ecclesiastical territory among themselves. In the auditorium the message came forth, "Judah shall plow" (Hos. 10:11). It was then interpreted that since "Judah" in Hebrew meant "praise," the praise or worship portion of the church service should be *"used"* to plow or prepare the minds and hearts of the people to receive the word or "seeds" given by preachers and teachers. Music is used in many ways (see chapter XIII), but "using," for other purposes, worship offered to God, is a desecration, a sacrilege, profaning something that is holy, separated unto God. Hosea 10:11, interpreted in its context, is a warning of judgment; that Judah will be enslaved in captivity.

What happened shortly after that prophetic word spread is that the publishing companies and writers of today's contemporary Christian worship music, whose property and services were used without compensation (Neh. 13:10) formed collectives and demanded royalty payments for the use of their material. "Spies" were sent out. If any copyrighted songs were being sung the church was "informed" that in a lawsuit they could lose money and/or their church property if they did not pay a yearly "fee." Some songs had to be avoided. Praise did indeed go into captivity. These collectives now collect millions of dollars for their "best hits" worship songs.

Singing songs that come from and convey the heart's desire has been replaced by staring at a bright light on a wall, reading words that used to be sung "by heart." If people would memorize a song, and thus not make or project a copy of it, there would be no infringement of rights of ownership. That is not too difficult or time consuming to do. Instead, today worship for many means staring toward bright lights on a wall and only singing the latest top twenty-five worship hits sung in many other churches in the country, each concert choreographed with the same dance steps learned from watching TV or YouTube.

Boundary disputes and battles over property ownership historically take place after revivals. The infringement of copyrights is also nothing new. The music of the Lutheran composer J. S. Bach was outlawed by the Catholic church. His Prelude #1 was at one time reported to be the Pope's favorite, but with words supplied by some creative nuns.

Worship should be a means of entering into the flowing stream of God's presence and partaking of His substance. This requires a gentle seeking spirit. It should not be a mechanistic use of simple repetitive words to control or motivate people, nor be taught as if it could impress or manipulate God. That use of music comes from a harsh, controlling spirit. How long will the captivity last? Is this mass-market organization, conformity, and uniformity of music in church the inevitable aftermath of revival?

X - The Song - Hope Triumphant

Before his parents died, Jonathan had dreams of singing in church. By the age of 10 he knew many of the Psalms by heart. One of his favorites was, "...that I might dwell in the house of the Lord all the days of my life, to behold the beauty of the Lord." After high school he got a job in the city and found a small apartment to share with some other guys.

That was not such a bad life. He found a church nearby and during the month people would gather at the apartment to discuss the Bible, to pray, and worship God. It was not like in his parent's old church of course, but still it felt good. He could continue to learn and dream of serving God.

That comfort was short lived. The room-mates who were the first ones to rent the apartment, only thought about partying. They began to object to church people hanging out at their place. Few came anymore. He missed his church family and his parents and prayed for God's help.

The only escape came when he went to his new church. Oh how he loved those services. He could listen to the teaching and try to remember the worship so he could repeat it later to remind himself that there was a God who cared for him and who had a better plan for him than stocking shelves at all hours day or night.

He remembered how his father and mother had both encouraged him to learn the Bible and follow Jesus. He remembered how they told him that one day he would stand before the congregation and he should expect to be touched by the Spirit of the Almighty. Something in him longed to sing Holy words with an anointing that came from Heaven.

Since he was only a part-timer, his work shift changed often. Working Sundays was required and he never knew if he would get to church. Soon he was at the store just about every Sunday. Then, one week, he had the day free and made his way to the worship, but got there late. To his surprise, special services were being held and the place was packed. He began to work his way slowly through the crowd until he found a seat up near the front.

He heard the one teaching say, "blessed are the meek for they shall inherit the earth," and "God is a Spirit: and they that worship him must worship him in Spirit and in Truth." It seemed as if he had never heard those words before, as though they reached out specifically to him. Each word sank deep into his soul. The love and compassion of God filled his being in a entirely new way.

The sermon was over and people began to leave. As the crowd thinned out the man whom they had all listened to turned and looked right at him and came to him. He put his hand on his head and said, "though you are still young Jonathan. You shall be a disciple of the Lord Jesus Christ and worship him. Truly, truly I tell you, You are the light of the world." Those words encircled his heart.

This time, walking back toward his lonely life, he was not struggling to remember encouraging words he had briefly heard others sing. This time there was a song bubbling up out of his own heart that he could barely contain, or even understand.

Words like, "Blessed be the Lamb of God," and "All Hail the King," formed wings of music out of his lips. What were the rest of the words to this new song he was singing? He had to go back and ask that visiting preacher to teach it all to him.

It was several weeks before he had another Sunday free. As the days passed the song in his heart grew stronger, the words clearer. He longed to get back to share it with the one who had touched him. When the day arrived, he practically ran to church.

He looked for a crowd, but it was just a typical quiet, almost empty service. He asked an usher, where he could find the one who taught last month, but was told he was in another city and would likely never be back to this small storefront church. Seeing the pain on Jonathan's face he spoke a little more kindly, "you might find him at a larger church or he may visit here if he has another free Sunday. it was just an accident that he came here last month."

Jonathan reeled at those words. "Just an accident?" The song was gone. In its place was a throbbing ache. Nothing mattered any more. He would never, could never, share the song and worship together with the one who had touched him so deeply. He wished he had never had that song in his heart.

He got through the rest of the service by habit, not thinking or feeling, but slowly, against everything he felt and knew, the song seemed to want to rise up and explode from within him. He held on.

As the end of the service approached and the communion was being passed Jonathan as usual reached for it. He did not see the usher who gave him the elements, but it seemed as though the man who handed him the bread had holes in his wrists. As he lifted the bread to his mouth a blinding light of glory shown around him.

Then, as he lifted the little cup to his lips he began to gave thanks, to worship, and Jonathan fell to his knees as the song burst forth out of his heart and mouth, "Glory To The One Who Died for me, The Risen Lamb of God, the King of Kings, the Messiah." Then the Lord vanished. But the simple song, born in the heart of a believer who had been touched by the Lord, was shared, heard, and received by God.

XI - The Emperor's New Band

Once upon a time there was an emperor who was widely known for his vanity. He thought himself to be very sophisticated and wise. He always wanted the very best and the very latest of everything.

Hearing about a troupe of troubadours newly arrived in his realm, he invited them to the castle. When they arrived they very humbly and sincerely apologized to the emperor because, although they themselves were nothing and of no reputation, their music was so refined and so new, it could only be understood, or even heard by those who were exceptionally spiritual as well as very wise.

Thinking himself to be both, the monarch gave them a bag of gold coins and said come back here next Sunday morning and perform for us. With that, he had scribes print leaflets to distribute throughout the realm to all those who were especially spiritual and wise, inviting them to participate in the event.

Wanting to be prepared, so that nothing went amiss, he stood outside the guest chambers to catch a bit of their rehearsal, but could not hear a thing, which troubled him greatly. Am I not as spiritual and wise as anyone, he thought. What shall I do Sunday morning? Well, no one else will hear anything then, anyway, so I might as well try to enjoy what I paid for.

The great day arrived and the auditorium was overflowing. The troubadours, again very humbly and sincerely presented themselves as being of no status or reputation, but explained that their music was only for the most select listeners, those who were both young in heart and yet discerning as the oldest sage; the most spiritual and the very wise.

They began to perform, or at least it seemed as if they began. Except for the one who was angrily beating a pot with two sticks, the others were moving their hands across lutes and harps, but making no sound from them. They all moved their lips as though singing, but nothing came out except an occasional belch. The emperor, not wanting to seem unwise, began to move his lips, hands, and feet in the same way the troubadours did. The guests, following his example, did likewise.

Up near the front sat an old couple with their young grandson. A few minutes into the show, he started laughing and cried out, "they're not making any music; they have no song." Respectable people nearby tried to both hush and excuse him at the same time, saying "he is too young to understand," but it was too late, the spell had been broken.

The other guests looked toward the emperor to see what to do, but he was hastily heading for an exit. All they could see was his backside, so they all left too. The troubadours packed up their melodyless instruments and their bag of gold coins and they also left.

* * * * * * *

What song do we have?

Turn your eyes upon Jesus, look full in His wonderful face..
When I survey the Wondrous cross.
The Head that once was crowned with thorns is crowned with glory now.
For I know that my Redeemer lives (Job 19:25).
Count your blessings see what God has done.
Jesus my Savior, Shepherd, Friend, my Prophet, Priest and King,
my Lord, my life, my way, my end, please accept the praise I bring.

Worship songs include, "I, me, my, mine, you, yours, we, ours, us, they or them" **but we are His**. Worship songs will clearly indicate a focus on our Lord Jesus Christ.

XII - The Story - Testimony

One of the blessings of being a minstrel is the chance to visit a variety of churches and hear the stories of the people. Everyone has a testimony. The best part is when they get to the line "...and then the Lord met me...," or "But God had other ideas for my life...." It doesn't stop there. Each day is a testimony of God's grace. We usually share just the highlights from our own life, or tell a story from the life of someone in our own family, church, denomination, or movement. Here's a story from the life of one, not too unusual, minstrel. The story is not over yet, nor the last song sung.

My father played coronet in an army band before I was born. My mother loved music too. There was often a radio playing in our apartment, usually classical music but sometimes, jazz, country, or folk music. My sister sang in the All-City choir. One of my uncles was a music teacher for many years at a mission school in New Mexico. My grandmother played piano for a church in rural Indiana. When I was five we spent the summer there and she taught me to play The *Star Spangled Banner* on the piano. Back home in the city, we didn't have a piano, but I did have an harmonica and a wooden recorder.

I sang in the glee club in elementary school, and in school plays. When I was ten my older sister got a guitar and I was sternly admonished never to touch it. Thus began my intensive practice. The following year I got a guitar too - and a record by Andres Segovia. I tried hard to figure out the notes he was playing but there were just too many of them.

I began playing guitar and leading sing-alongs around campfires in the Boy Scouts when I was 12 or 13. By the time I was in high school I was leading marches to camp playing the banjo. I didn't know it then, but I was following a long line of musicians who since colonial times led marches and singing at rallies of patriots, abolitionists, suffragettes, union organizers, pro- and anti-war advocates, this or that side during political campaigns – and for worship.

I began to study at the Brooklyn Conservatory of Music while I was in high school and later played and sang in coffee houses. In college I pestered a professor, an excellent jazz and classical guitarist, until he taught me to read and play the classical guitar music I loved. I learned a little jazz and some history too. My technique and my instruments and my equipment were never the best, but I didn't let that stop me. I never let ignorance of the words, melody, or rhythm, stop me either. If ya gotta sing, ya gotta sing.

After two years, I dropped out of college and explored the world a bit. I had affirmed my faith in Christ at a church when I was 14, but I met the Lord and was born again 5 years later at a Christian commune outside of Brownsville, Oregon. Soon after, at a convention in Eugene, I followed my friends into a little room up front so as not to lose my ride back to the farm. Somebody put their hands on my head and I went down, praising the Lord in tongues, with a face splitting smile on my face that didn't go away for three days. I got dunked (baptized) in the river the next day. I had no idea what was going on. Thinking to do the right thing I went back East and finished college.

Three years after graduating I realized there was a need for a foundation in my life so I enrolled in a Bible college. My music was enthusiastically welcomed at first. After the second try they said please don't play anymore. Aside from a little Bach I did not know any Christian worship music. Because of my banjo I got drafted to work in Sunday school with the kids. This was the Lord's way of teaching me the Sunday school lessons I had missed growing up in a secular home. I must have played **Rise and Shine and Give God the Glory** 10,000 times. I can still count kangaroozies by twozies in my sleep.

At Bible college I spent time in the Word and with the Lord. After laying down my own efforts I began to learn the ways of the Lord. He spoke to me and sang to me. I learned to wait upon th Lord, to sense the anointing, His presence, and the leading of the Holy Spirit. Near the end of school He anointed me with a thermo-nuclear explosion from which I have not recovered. That day and the next ones following seemed ordinary enough, but things began to happen like never before and before any thought or move on my part. I was just worshiping the Lord.

The doors of ministry began to open: leading worship in small prayer groups, leading chorus singing at evening church meetings, and while visiting in institutions such as jails, nursing homes, hospitals, and colleges. The Lord enabled me to form evangelistic singing groups of college students and a choir of adults with cognitive impairments. After pastoring a small church a call came to lead worship at a larger church and to teach some Bible.

When doors of full-time traveling evangelism opened. I traveled throughout North America sharing in small groups and large. Later the call came to go to France. At first I spoke little French but I could sense the presence and moving of the Holy Spirit when worshiping and providing music for a prayer group. He led and I followed. It was more fun to lead worship that way than to learn French.

One Sunday I got drafted to play at church when the pianist was sick. The French use the Sofage method for chords and use a more minor tonality. The worship leader was in such a hurry. What a job it was to try to understand the French *and the music*. What a blessing it is to simply follow the leading of the Holy Ghost. He leads and I follow.

I have never been paid or gone anywhere with a contract. I have received shelter, food, clothing, old cars and gas. I worked a variety of jobs to survive, to pay my way along the way, but overall, the Lord is my portion.

After I returned to America a particular story seemed especially poignant to me. A missionary returning to the United States got off the airplane and after customs inspection sat waiting for his ride to show up. There was a group celebrating the arrival of a famous person, either a politician, a movie star, or maybe a rock musician. There were banners, balloons, and a band. Off to one side the missionary was feeling very alone, alienated, and a stranger in his own country. In a bout of self-pity he thought, "there is no welcome celebration here for me, I guess my life is not that important." Just then the Lord spoke to him and said, "My son, these people are celebrating their homecoming. You are not home yet."

What a time of worship that homecoming will be. Listen! When We All Get To Heaven, Draw Me Nearer, Give Me Jesus, What A Fellowship, When The Roll Is Called and The Saints Go Marching In. I'll be there, Just As I Am. Amazing Grace, Grace Enough For Me. There IS Power In The Blood. What A Savior, The Rock Of Ages, though nailed to The Old Rugged Cross, He Lifted Me, to Higher Ground. Glory To God He Lifted Me Up. Oh For A Thousand Tongues To Sing, Praise The Name Of Jesus, I Will Praise Him, To God Be The Glory. Great things He has done. And that worship will last for eternity!

* * * * * * * *

The songs we sing can fit into categories. Some are love songs, praise and worship songs, or consecration songs that speak of a desire to know God more or to follow him more closely. There are scripture songs, songs full of sound doctrine, and those that tell a gospel story. What we sing, and who we sing to reveals our heart. Jesus taught, it is better to address God with monosyllabic colloquialisms rather than with tautological idiomatic verbosity (that is, don't use vain repetition – Matthew. 6:7).

Some songs simply say: Jesus is God, He is good, Lah dee dah, He loves me, Lah dee dah, I love him, Lah dee dah, dee dah. I listened to one like that the other day. It was almost embarrassing for the first 30 seconds. Then the Lord came and anointed it with His presence. I think He did that because the person who wrote and sang it, though unskilled, had a heart to know and to follow after God. That makes all the difference. What the heart sings the voice can only try to express.

There is also special anointing on the worship and songs that come from sacrifice and suffering. From the stoning of Stephen in Acts chapter seven, to the wars of the reformation, or the slaughter of Christians in Nazi Germany, or the Soviet Union, China, Uganda, Rwanda or Iraq, the songs of the martyrs are very special. So too are the songs of worship that arise out of personal loss and grief. One day we may get to hear them all.

XIII. How to Describe Music

The conversation of our lives is our worship (Phil. 1:27). God is most concerned with that. Mercy, truth, holiness, kindness, humility, wisdom, justice, self-control, perseverance, faith, hope, and love are the sacrifices of worship most pleasing to our God (Psalm. 51:15-17, Matt. 9:13, 12:7, 15:9, John 9:31, James 1:27, I John. 3:18). He enjoys that music. A more narrow definition of worship points to a ritualistic, temple-like, worship with a focus on things like singing, dancing, instruments, and raising hands (I Chron. 16: 4 22, 27, 29).

Some churches prohibit musical instruments in the service. Others have a director of music with a well trained orchestra and a choir or two. Often any musical talent is welcomed. This, sadly, includes worshipers and leaders who are unsaved or barely saved. Even those who are in gross sin may be given positions of leadership solely because of talent. Allowing a person to participate in an activity can be a tool of evangelization, and a means of nurturing and working with someone. However, both the person and the music are vehicles which carry and impart something. Discernment and caution should be observed.

The minstrel and the music may bring healing or deliverance. They may soothe and calm anger and agitation (I Sam. 16:23, II Kings 3:15). They may help move a person to touch or be touched by God. Music paves the way toward relaxing, or working, reconciliation, or fighting. It can lead to rejoicing, or open the healing floodgates of weeping during mourning to bring much needed comfort (Matt. 9:23).

In addition to the *words*, the *spirit*, the *purpose*, and the *life lived*, questions are often raised about what music itself is. Music is a gift from God. What we do with it is our gift to God. Some groups only sing hymns, others only sing short choruses. The use of contemporary tunes, by Charles Wesley and Thomas Dorsey is cited as examples to prove the potential for God's claim on or even approval on any contemporary music which is then labeled good just because it is new. That "Contemporaneity Rule" is a theory that the "new" is the only effective interpreter of the present and thus the greatest change agent for "now." It was developed by a secular psychologist and adopted by some Christians. The old Gospel is still the most effective change agent, but claims that "anything goes," too often go unanswered.

Situations vary but *standards exist*--both Biblical standards and musical standards. Spiritual reality is not merely subjective. The Bible and the church have much to say concerning valid spiritual reality. There are some, but not many different interpretations of the scriptures. What the Word says and means is not confusing. There may be battles over a particular application. The same is true of music. It is not judged or considered only from a subjective viewpoint. Standards can be ignored, or applied, or misapplied. They may be turned into law, or handled with grace. Politics, power, tradition, or necessity may rule. The thing to be aware of and to affirm is that **standards for music do exist**. How they are handled and what priorities are set, or are even possible is another issue.

Music can be described or felt in terms of its: 1) orchestration; what instruments and/or voices are used, 2) dynamics; is it loud or soft, 3) the pitch; high or low part of a scale, 4) the tune or melody: the movement; spacing and tempo of notes, the direction of the melody notes up and down, 5) the harmony, or the combination of notes and chords, and 6) the rhythm and beat. A very important quality observed about these elements is called TENSION, and the release of tension. This is what makes music so emotionally attractive. This is why it can move us to cheers or tears. Each of these elements produces some tension. The skillful balance, blending and altering of these elements creates "good" music.

Rock & Roll has many offshoots and variations but can be described as: music which uses rhythmic tension created by a beat. It typically uses 1) drums, bass, rhythm and lead guitar with 2) loud volume and little variation in dynamics. 3) Pitch change is abrupt rather than part of a melody. 4) The tempo is rapid, with large gaps or jumps, rather than notes being connected with melodic lines or scales, and the direction is usually ascending, rising and repetitious. 5) The harmony is usually a repetitive bass line with a major or minor interval. 6) The rhythm is very fast 4/4 time, and the beat dominates. The **tension** rarely varies and is not released until the music stops. The consistent way these musical elements are blended makes Rock & Roll easy to identify. It is like a cake with most of the ingredients and flavors minimized or absent leaving only one or two exaggerated and dominating.

Whether any one individual likes it or not, or calls it "good," and how it effects a person or people may be a personal or group statement. Some people enjoy a diet high in sugar, salt, and fat, others may like to read only certain books. Those are personal not cultural preferences. The analysis of a music form, even though there are many variations of that form, is not subjective. All music of a certain category does not have to fit all the criteria of this analysis. These are general statements which are more or less accurate descriptions. Music is described using objective standards and evaluated as to the blending of these elements, as well as how it effects people.

As long ago as 1558, Gioseffo Zarlino, a philosopher of the late Renaissance, noticed that melodies using a major 3rd above the tonic sounded cheerful and melodies with a minor 3rd sounded sad. Over 400 years later the felt experience of major and minor chords is the same or similar. Some types, and even keys of music are considered triumphant, joyful, sad, romantic, or sensual in nature. In countries where witchcraft and animism are practiced, some people have discovered that the beat of Rock & Roll music is similar to the drum beat used by witch doctors to call up evil spirits. These factors are fairly consistent over time and between cultures even though all individuals do not relate and react to them in exactly the same way.

* * * * * * * *

Sensing the presence of God requires the cultivation of our spiritual senses of discernment. These can be overwhelmed by physical senses. Music and song lyrics can touch us in ways that open us to perceive and relate to God, or they can overshadow the still small voice of God.

A physical beat, a sensuous melody or music, or lyrics that completely saturate the mind and soul may block our hearing God's voice. They can also become idols, perceived and labeled as the presence of God when they are merely physical sensations, or human emotions or thoughts. Physical vibrations and lighting sensations can cloud the senses. Young people are especially susceptible to sensory stimulation both in the physical and the spiritual and those who are aware of this may use it to manipulate them. We are first in the natural. then in the spiritual (I Cor. 15:46). The flesh wars against the spirit and the spirit against the flesh (Gal. 5:16-26).

XIV. The Uses of Music

Music is used for many natural purposes:

Communication: the lyrics of a song may convey a Gospel message, a prayer or prophecy, or tell a story, or share an emotion or an experience.

Education: material may be easier to teach, or learn, or memorize when put to music, such as with scripture songs or hymns full of doctrine.

Entertainment: sporting events or meetings and conferences are made more exciting, emotional and attractive by the use of music.

Exercise, the rhythms of music are useful for aerobic workouts, dancing, working, or keeping awake and alert while driving.

Unity: songs that are common to a group bind them together, such as our national anthem, songs from our past, or our shared holiday songs.

Branding: advertisers try to get a melody or a song closely identified with the name of an organization, business, or product so customers remember it.

Control: music can move people to action or to inaction in ways that are predictable, such as when marching in step or waiting for time to pass.

Focus attention: music can direct people's attention, announce arrival, indicate where to go or what to do, and attract or disperse a crowd.

Comfort and healing: music can be therapeutic and soothe emotions, or relieve stress, and it may minister healing and deliverance.

Calm and rest: music can help people relax by affecting blood pressure, and heart rate, and it can redirect or distract attention and calm anger.

Personal gain: music may increase self-esteem, status and power and it may lead to financial gain and/or individual or group fulfillment.

Worship: music may be used in exulting, which is a triumphant, lively expression of joy in God, and it can be used in exalting, that is, extolling the virtues of God. Music can help people focus on and touch God and be touched by God. It may be a means to connect with God the Father, God the Son, and God the Holy Spirit. The highest purpose of music is Anointed Spiritual Prophetic Kingdom Worship. Such an updraft occurs when the presence of God manifests.

The flowering of music into prophetic Spiritual Kingdom worship requires an uplifting or upsurge from heaven, from God. This is not a natural process such as increased volume. It is Holy, a set-apart-for-God service. Not all Christians can or will cultivate their relationship with God using music. A worshipful relationship with God can grow through other activities such as, Bible reading, or prayer, or acts of service such as gardening. See chapter XV for other Spiritual Disciplines.

The flowering of music into prophetic Spiritual Kingdom worship, requires gifting, grace, and growth from God. Not everyone desires this or believes this exists. Conflict over the uses of music may seem to be over personal taste or style, or culture, or generational differences. It may instead be about natural music supplanting Spiritual worship, not contemporary versus traditional. Our Adamic nature wants to hide from or control God, but God will guide us if we allow Him Lordship of our life.

Worship in Spirit and in Truth requires cultivating a desire for more of God and less of self (John 3:30). Desiring that He be Lord. The desire of our heart, more than our taste in music leads and flavors our worship. We need to pray that our worship comes from a heart that desires God's likeness grow in us; where his gentleness, compassion, love, kindness, humility, patience, and forgiveness are growing and thankfulness to God abounds. Such a heart will point to and lift up Jesus. We need to also pray for discernment.

Growing into the image of Jesus is helped by the gift of discernment from the Holy Spirit who points to the truth and quickens, makes alive, the scripture. We find in the Bible a more intimate revelation of God; our brother, our Bridegroom, our Lord Jesus Christ, God the Son, God the Holy Spirit, God the Father, the Three who are the One true God we worship.

A worship service is not just a time to sing at or about God. Songs reflect, but also create our heart attitude and aim. We may listen to each other when we sing. Listen also to what God is saying to us through songs. Worship can be an important time for having two-way communion and fellowship with God.

Worship services that are concerts can be entertaining, even educational. A congregation hearing each other singing together can foster unity. The natural uses of music may lead to Anointed, Spiritual, Prophetic, Kingdom Worship in the manifest presence of God. Aim high.

We do not have to use a certain style, or type of music for worship, or evangelism, or for church planting or building. These things are not accomplished by "(human) might, or (human) power, but by My Spirit says the Lord (Zechariah 4:6). The Holy Spirit points to the truth (John 16:13). He anoints worship that is directed to Jesus who is the Truth (John 14:6). The Holy Spirit gives birth to and witnesses to musical worship that reveals Jesus. He often anoints that type of song to the level of Spiritual worship.

When Jesus is lifted up He draws people to Himself (John 12:32). The anointing breaks bondage and brings liberty (II Corinthians 3:17). There is more going on than just singing songs.

The Holy Spirit may empower an existing musical expression we create, but songs do not only have a human source. Anointed songs may originate from the Father, Son, or Holy Spirit. Anointed songs always have life, but when directed by God through a submitted vessel to a specific person, people, or setting, they have a powerful affect.

Prophetic worship may echo worship in heaven or witness the Holy Spirit's intent to bring edification, exhortation, and comfort. God has a message for us. He can reveal what is real or show us things to come through song. A song can be intercessory prayer or be Spiritual warfare. It may convict of sin or reveal the desire and condition of our hearts –if we listen to the voice of our singing God. Aim high!

* * * * * * * *

We usually choose why we use music and how we use technology in church. During one gathering, the sound system blew a fuse, but the members of the worship team were experienced troupers. They kept right on worshiping the Lord. Amazingly, without the amplified instruments, we could hear the words of the songs. Without amplified singers we could hear each other sing. What a different atmosphere. This was **corporate worship**, not just a concert by a praise band.

A couple of hours later a sign was projected on the screen which said, **"Childcare will be ending in 10 minutes. Please pick up your Child."** The 12 word message was in large letters that filled the entire screen so everyone could see it. The song lyrics projected earlier were all in small text tightly squeezed into the center of the screen, probably just taken off the Internet with little thought for what format would be easier to see.

What a difference this makes. **The songs we sing communicate a message which we want people to know. The way we present them and how we worship, sends a message about who we worship and who we want to reach and who we want to include or to exclude and who we intend to share the good news with and who we intend to ex- communicate.**

Unnecessarily excluding people from church is harming them. Misuses of technology may also cause physical harm. A decibel (db) meter, or Sound Pressure Level (SPL) meter, able to measure 30 db to 130 db, may cost $10 to $60. There are SPL apps for smart phones. The accuracy of different sound meters may vary by as much as 20 db. Exposure to 100 db of sound should be avoided to avoid damage to hearing. *Wearing ear plugs in church is now a mandatory safety precaution in many churches.*

Approximate font sizes   John 3:16 (NKJV)

(Arial 12 point font)
(14 point)
(16 point)
(18 point)
(24)
(36)

For God so loved the world that He gave His only begotten Son, that whoever believes in Him should not perish

but have
everlasting life.

If the church projection or bulletin or what comes over the sound system is important, let it be clearly and safely seen and heard!

A - How to Use Technology In Worship

We can increase sizes of projected, printed, or Internet text with our churches' computers. The tendency is to just use what is habit or preset and this means smaller fonts and more words. Small print bulletins, Bibles, or sermon outlines are hard to read, especially in a poorly lit sanctuary. We could instead choose to communicate songs, scriptures, or messages in the most readable format, not small text, and without confusing pictures, designs, movement, and without poor letter/background color contrast.

Inclusive use of computers could help some of the 25 million Americans (about 8% or 1 in 12) who report they cannot see well even with glasses (source: The National Health Interview Survey, 2008, www.cdc.gov/nchs/nhis.htm). It could also help some of the 40 million non-disabled, English speaking Americans, age 16 and older (14% or 1 in 8) who cannot read at a basic literacy level (source: NAAL at www.nces.ed.gov).

The Biblical reasons for using computers inclusively are very clearly stated, (1) Do not curse the deaf or put a stumbling block in front of the blind (Lev. 19:14), (2) Cursed is the man who leads the blind astray (Deut. 27:18), also see (3) whatever you did for one of the least of these brothers of mine, you did for me (Matt 25:40), (4) look not only to your own interests, but also to the interests of others (Phil. 2:4), (5) we who are strong ought to bear with the failings of the weak and not to please ourselves (Ro. 15:1).

The Gospels reveal that people were antagonistic toward those who could not see well, who requested help (Matt. 20:31; 21:15; Mk. 10:48; Lk 18:39; Jn 9:28, 34). In sharp contrast, Jesus cared about what they wanted and had compassion on them (Matt. 20:32; Mk. 10:49; Lk. 18:40; Jn. 9:1). Jesus also sought feedback about the help He gave. He asked if His efforts were successful and when He found they were not, Jesus went a little further, prayed a little longer, and did a little more (Mark 8:23-26).

Most of us cannot heal blindness, but we can help people see by the way we use our computers. That choice is ours. Regrettably, just as in Biblical times, many have chosen to create stumbling blocks instead of allowing people to see, even though we believe love does not harm its neighbor (Rom. 13:10). Waiting until someone asks for help means that barriers will remain and even increase in our church. We know what Jesus did. It takes a few extra minutes to learn to use computers in a way that creates the most readable text on screen and on paper. It is not difficult or expensive. **Begin a little at a time, maybe one song or part of a bulletin each week. After some practice it will be easily done.**

B - Optimum Readability of Projected, Printed, or Internet Text

Projection: It is easiest to read projected text if the contrast is a solid, medium-blue background with plain, yellow or white letters. Consult a Color Contrast Wheel Online to find other contrasting colors. It is harder to read projected text if the background has objects, shading, areas of bright light, dark and light areas, patterns, pictures, multiple colors, lines, or if it has movement in it.

It is easiest to read projected text with only about 15 words per screen. They should still be a meaningful chunk of words, with the font as large as possible, so it fills the entire screen. Projected text is easier to read with only one type of font with even thickness (san serif fonts), expanded to 1.1. letter and line spacing. It is harder to read text if the letters, words, and lines are condensed, or if the letters are uneven, thin, fancy, or with appearance affects such as, italic, cursive, bold, outline, underline, shadow, or all caps.

Printed Material: Large print text is 18 point font (source: the American Foundation for the Blind). Standard print is 12 point font, but some churches print bulletins in even smaller font. The best contrast for printed material is black ink on solid yellow or white paper. It is hard to read dark ink on a dark background, or light ink on dark paper, or on paper or an e-mail or Website that has pictures, patterns, multiple colors, shading, or lines.

Readability is best with a plain sans serif font, such as Arial, without appearance affects and without condensing the letters, words, or lines. A few dozen large print (16 to 18+ or even 35 to 72 point font) newsletters, outlines, tracts, bulletins, Gospels, or handouts on 8½" by 14" paper folded in half are not costly.

Bibles: Bible-publishers create definitions for the terms, "large," "extra large," or "giant" print in terms of their own standard size print. These are not true large print. Bookstore employees unaware of this issue might inadvertently mislead customers. A truly large print (18 point font) Bible in one volume is only available in a King James version and a New King James version. Other versions in one volume in truly large print could be made if people requested them. Bible software programs allow for text enlargement and color and contrast change. Ebook devices allow for font size change, but that may not be large enough if they have little or no color or contrast or lighting control. Alternatives to reading exist, such as a Bible on tape or CD, but holding and reading the Bible is often preferred to listening to it or to using a computer.

The Internet: On a Website or e-newsletter allow the text to "wrap" or "reflow" so that zooming will enlarge the text without extending it beyond the screen sides. Use good color contrast and avoid textured wall-paper or text on pictures. Pictures and links need labels and do not use pop-ups.

C - Those Who Have Ears to Hear
Let Them Hear!

A major survey found that there are about **8,000,000 people** in the United States, **(3.7% of the population)** over 5 years of age who are hard of hearing (they reported some difficulty hearing normal conversation even with the use of a hearing aid). More than half of those were over 65 years of age. Another survey found there are more than **28,000,000 people (that is almost 10% of the population)** who reported "a little trouble" hearing, (without the use of a hearing aids). More than half of those were over 45 years of age (source: Ross Mitchell, Gallaudet Research Institute, Gallaudet University, 2011).

According to the 2012 Canadian Survey on Disability (CSD) by Statistics Canada, there are almost one million (959,590) people with a vision loss in Canada, The Canadian Hearing Society (CHS, 2013), reports one million Canadians have a hearing related disability and nine million adults (over one-fourth of the population) have some hearing loss, According to CHS, some studies indicate the true number may be three million or more adults with a hearing related disability because those with hearing problems will often under-report their condition.

There are almost two million people in the United Kingdom with sight loss (National Health Statistics, 2013). About 3.5 million people of working age (16 to 65 years) are "deaf or hard of hearing." However, almost ten million people in the UK have "some degree of hearing impairment or deafness" according to Action On Hearing Loss (2014).

An Ear Loop System in an auditorium works with hearing aids which have a telecoil (about half of all the hearing aids in use have this). An ear loop System costs about $1,000 to $2,000 depending on who installs it, and the size of the area covered, and the number of additional receivers purchased to lend to those without compatible hearing aids. Many small to medium sized houses of worship with less than a 500 seat auditorium install an ear loop system cost-effectively with in-house talent. Installation is not difficult and should not be expensive. There are a half dozen Ear Loop System companies with easy to find Websites. An Fm or Infrared system may work for a smaller church.

Not everyone communes with God in musical worship.

Consider the 24 Spiritual Disciplines in the next chapter.

XV - 24 Spiritual Disciplines

A simple definition of a "Spiritual Discipline" is a habit or regular pattern in life that intensifies our focus on God. Spiritual disciplines are doorways learned from our Lord Jesus Christ, the Bible, and the Church and are empowered by the Holy Spirit. The 24 terms on this list may seem self-explanatory, but each has various meanings. Each one can be the focus of one discussion, and/or one practice time or several, but may still require years of practice in order to enter into it individually as led by God. It can help to discuss our successes and failures with practicing spiritual disciplines with a friend, or mentor, or in a small group (see problems and misconceptions on page 50).

Prayer - adoring, thanksgiving, confessing, interceding, and petitioning.

Creating Sacred Space - doing this gives a place for other disciplines!

Bible Reading - devotionally, prayerfully, reciting memorizing, as well as studying.

Singing - singing unto God Psalms, hymns, spiritual songs, and choruses.

Quiet Time - waiting quietly on the Lord and just being with the Lord.

Divine Guidance - listening to, hearing from, and being led by God.

Meditation / Contemplation - focusing attention on Jesus Christ.

Journaling - writing about times or days with God or writing to God.

Testimony & Storytelling - sharing what God has done or is doing.

Daily Devotions - special readings or other activities not on this list.

Sabbath Observation - attending church and changing the week's routine.

Giving - tithing, money, time, talents to support Christian activity and alms giving.

Gifting - seeking, cultivating, and practicing the gifts of the Holy Spirit.

Fasting - giving up food, drink, or things like Tv or computers for a time.

Loneliness / Solitude - with God who is everywhere present.

Suffering - (crisis or chronic) with God who is all powerful.

Peril - facing danger or risking loss with God who is all knowing.

Patience - waiting, enduring, restraining self with God who is eternal.

Self-denial / Sacrifice - controlling self and giving at a loss to self.

Simplicity - simplifying life and lifestyle - begin by simplifying this list!

Service - hospitality, volunteering, helping (seen or unseen by others).

Sharing - being a friend, a neighbor, building relationships, visiting shut-ins.

Evangelization and Outreach - distributing tracts, New Testaments sharing the Gospel, inviting and bringing people to church, Bible teaching.

Resting - allowing God to minister peace and rest to you; slowing down, napping, sleeping, taking a vacation or a restful spiritual retreat

Common problems with practicing Spiritual Disciplines include:

Procrastination (waiting until tomorrow or some better time to begin).

Distractions (interruptions by thoughts, and things, activities, or people).

Giving up too soon (when results do not come as soon as desired).

Expecting specific results (as if in doing this we are bargaining with God).

Never changing them (not personalizing them, or getting stuck in a rut).

There are many false ideas about practicing Spiritual Disciplines. The following list of things that are **NOT TRUE** has to be mentioned because of the fact that *practice is not the performance and boot camp is not the battle.*

Common misconceptions about Spiritual Disciplines that are NOT TRUE include:

X Anyone can do these, anytime, and should.

X These are what it means to be a Christian.

X Spiritual Disciplines must be done in order to be a Christian.

X They can be effectually done apart from the enabling grace of God.

X Practicing Spiritual Disciplines makes a person a more mature Christian.

X One discipline, or one person's way of practicing a Spiritual Discipline is more spiritual than another.

The rewards of practicing Spiritual Disciplines are a greater enjoyment of God and each other and living a more fulfilling and fruitful life.

Helpful aids to find and use include:

The many scriptures that specifically relate to each Spiritual Discipline.

Songs related to Spiritual Disciplines for group and individual singing

Additional books, articles, pictures, or poetry about particular disciplines.

Books on Spiritual Discipleship:

The Pursuit of God, by A. W. Tozer, (find it Online at: www.theboc.com/freestuff/awtozer/ books/the_pursuit_of_god/)

Hinds Feet in High Places, by Hannah Hurnard,

The Practice of the Presence of God, by Brother Lawrence,

My Utmost For His Highest, by Oswald Chambers,

Being Made Ready: A Daily Devotional, by Wade E. Taylor (find it at www.wadetaylorpublications.org).

Of the Imitation of Christ, by Thomas à Kempis, (find it Online at: www.manybooks.net/titles/kempisthetext99mcrst11.html

Purity of Heart Is To Will One Thing, by Sören Kierkegaard, (find it Online at: www.religion-online.org/showbook.asp?title=2523

Other aids as discovered or created by each Christian disciple. This outline on Spiritual Discipline is not exclusive or exhaustive. It is gleaned from various sources over many years and is still growing.

Some scriptures on Spiritual Discipline

Prov. 3:5-6: Trust in the Lord with all your heart and lean not on your own understanding. In all your ways acknowledge him, and he shall

direct your paths.

Prov. 8:17, I love them that love me; and those that seek me early shall find me.

Jer. 29:13, You will seek me and find me when you seek me with all your heart.

Mt. 11:28-29: Come to me, ... learn from me,... Mk. 2:14,...Follow me.

Lk. 9:23: deny (yourself) and. . . take up (your) cross daily . . ..

Jn. 5:30 & Jn.15:5: By myself I can do nothing . . .

 apart from me you can do nothing

Gal. 3:3, After beginning with the Spirit, are you now trying to attain your goal by human effort?

Phil. 3:10: I want to know Christ and the power of his resurrection and the fellowship of sharing in his sufferings, becoming like him in his death.

* * * * * * * *

Some Scriptures on Worship

Clap

Psalm 47:1

Dance

Ps. 149:3

Ps. 150:4

Harp(s)

I Sam. 16:23

I Kings 10:12

I Chr. 16:5

I Chr. 25:1&3

II Chr. 20:28

II Chr. 29:25

Ne. 12:27

Ps. 137:2

Rev. 14:2, 15:2

Holiness

Ps. 29:2

Ps. 32:11,

Ezek. 33:32

I Pet. 2:9

James 1:26, 2:8, 3:9-10

Hymn(s)

Matt. 26:30

Eph. 5:19

Col. 3:16

Instruments

II Sam. 6:5

I Chr. 15:16

I Chr. 16:42

I Chr. 23:5

II Chr. 5:13

II Chr. 7:6

II Chr. 30:21

II Chr. 34:12

Ps. 68:25, 150:4

Isa. 38:20

Leap

Lk. 6:23

Melody

Isa. 51:3

Amos 5:23

Minstrel(s)

II Kings. 3:15

Matt. 9:23

Praise

Gen. 29:35

Judges. 5:3

I Chr. 16:4,

23:30, 29:13

II Chr. 20:19

Psalm: 7:17,

22:22, 22:26,

28:7, 30:9,

30:12, 33:1

33:2, 34:1,

42:5, 43:5,

51:15, 56:4,

74:21, 86:12,

100:1, 100:4,

106:2, 106:12,

107:31, 111:1,

113:9, 119:164,

138:2, 139:14,

145:4, 150:6

Isa. 38:18-19,

42:8, 43:21,

60:18, 61:3

Jer. 33:11

Joel 2:26

Matt. 21:16

Lk.18:43,

Lk. 19:37

Jn. 12:43

Ro. 2:29, 15:11

Phil. 1:11, 4:8

Heb. 2:12

Heb. 13:15

Sang

II Chr. 29:28

II Chr. 29:30

Ezra 3:11

Acts 16:25

Shout
II Chr. 13:15
Ezra 3:11,13
Ps. 5:11, 35:27
Zech. 9:9

Singing
I Sam. 18:6
I Chr. 6:32
I Chr. 13:8
II Chr. 23:18
Ezra 2:65
Ps. 100:2
Ps. 126:2
Isa. 51:11
Isa. 54:1
Zeph. 3:17

Sing Praises
Ex. 15:11
Ps. 9:11,22:3,
27:6, 47:6,&7,
68:4, 108:3,
146:2, 147:1,
149:6,

Song
Ex. 15:2
Deut. 31:21
I Chr. 15:22
I Chr. 25:6

II Chr. 29:27
Ps. 18:1, 28:7,
33:3, 40:3,
42:8, 69:30,
77:6, 96:1,
108:1, 118:14,

Songs
I Chr. 25:7
Job 35:10
Ne. 12:46
Ps. 32:7
Ps. 119:54
Ps. 137:3,:4
Ps. 144:9
Ps. 149:1
Isa. 12:2
Isa. 35:10
Ezek. 26:13

Worship
Ex. 34:14
I Chr. 9:33
I Chr. 16:29
I Chr. 23:13
Ps. 95:6
Dan. 3:28
Matt. 4:10
Matt. 15:9
John 4:23. 24
Phil. 3:3

Heb. 1:6
Rev. 4:10
Rev. 5:9
Rev. 14:3,
Rev. 14: 7, 11,
Rev. 15:4
Rev. 19:5, 10
Rev. 22:8, 9

Part II - Music Theory and Technique
For The Acoustic Guitar pgs. 55 - 79
practice, practice, practice, study, study, study

The Notes On The Guitar

The Nut (open strings)

	6 E	5 A	4 D	3 G	2 B	1 E
1st fret	F	A#(B♭)	D#	G#	C	F
2nd fret	F#	B	E	A	C#	F#
3rd fret	G	C	F	A#(B♭)	D	G
4th fret	G#	C#	F#	B	D#	G#
5th fret	A	D	G	C	E	A
6th fret	A#(B♭)	D#	G#	C#	F	A#
7th fret	B	E	A	D	F#	B
8th fret	C	F	A#(B♭)	D#	G	C
9th fret	C#	F#	B	E	G#	C#
10th fret	D	G	C	F	A	D
11th fret	D#	G#	C#	F#	A#(B♭)	D#
12th fret	E	A	D	G	B	E

Chord Boxes

Guitarists often use pictures or fingering codes instead of reading music notation on the staff. Tablature is a picture of the strings on the neck (held sideways). The numbers on the lines (strings) tell at which fret to press (just behind the fret) and the letters on top tell which finger of the left hand to use to press the string. A chord box is a variation of this. It represents a portion of the guitar neck and tells what fingers to use and where to put them.

The numbers in the box tell what finger of the left hand to use: index finger is 1, middle = 2, ring = 3, and the pinky is # 4. An x = do not play, o = play the open string, a = alternate bass. If x,o,a, are not given play the uncovered strings only if they sound good with the chord. If no fret position is given assume it is at the nut, or in first position.

E Chord

strings	6	5	4	3	2	1		o
		o	o					
1st fret					1			
2nd fret		2	3					
3rd fret								

Am Chord

	6	5	4	3	2	1
	a	o				o
1st fret					1	
2nd fret			2	3		
3rd fret						

C Chord

	x	o		o		
1st fret					1	
2nd fret			2			
3rd fret		3				

D Chord

	x	a	o			
1st fret						
2nd fret				1		2
3rd fret					3	

A Chord

	a	o			o	
1st fret						
2nd fret			1	2	3	
3rd fret						

G Chord

			o	o	o	
1st fret						
2nd fret		1				
3rd fret	2					3

Em Chord

o   o o o

	1	2		

o   E7   o

			1	
	2	3		
				4

x   C7   o

				1
		2		
	3		4	

a o A7 o   o

		1		3

a o A7

		1	1	1
					2

Dm Chord

x a

| | | | | | 1
|---|---|---|---|---|
| | | | 2 | |
| | | 4 | | 3 |

o   Em7 o   o

	1	2		
				4

a   B7   o

		1		
	2		3	
					4

x a o D7

				1
			2	
					3

a o Am7

				1
		2	3	
					4

The chords are placed in a certain order on the preceding pages in order to highlight certain patterns or **Chord Shapes** that repeat and are useful.

1) E is a step - ⌐, or backward L, (so is Am).

2) C is a slanted line - / (Dm is a slant with a brace Λ, just like C7).

[The D chord is the same shape as the strings 3, 2, 1, of the C chord. The D note is 2 frets higher than the C note, so the three notes (of the D chord) are moved up two frets. The D chord can be viewed as a v or y shape.]

3) A is a strait line - –, (so is Em).

Bar Chords

The technique called barring, or using bar chords, is to use the side of the first finger to press down two or more (up to all six) strings as if the nut was moving up and shortening the neck. Next the chord pattern is placed under that bar. The patterns above (and others) are **moved up or down the neck** to produce different chords. It is important to remember the order of the notes on the neck of the guitar. Moving a chord, up or down ½ step (1 fret), or more, changes the chord. For example: an E chord moved up 1 fret, under a bar, becomes an F chord.

(E moved up 1 fret) = an F chord

1st fret	1	1	1	1	1	1
2nd fret				2		
3rd fret		3	4			

(E moved up 3 frets) = G

3rd fret	1	1	1	1	1	1
4th fret				2		
5th fret		3	4			

(A moved up 1 fret) = B♭ (B flat)

1st fret	1	1	1	1	1	1
2nd fret						
3rd fret			2	3	4	

(partial bar with E at 1st fret) = F

1st fret					1	1
2nd fret				2		
3rd fret		3	4			

(partial bar with E at 3rd fret) = G

3rd fret					1	1
4th fret				2		
5th fret		3	4			

(partial bar with A at 1st fret) = B♭

1st fret						1
2nd fret						
3rd fret			2	3	4	

(A moved up 3 frets) =   C chord

3rd fret	1	1	1	1	1	1
4th fret						
5th fret			2	3	4	

© moved up 2 frets) = D

2nd fret	1	1	1	1	1	1
3rd fret					2	
4th fret			3			
5th fret		4				

The C shape (/) is rarely moved up this way. It is usually the D shape (V or y) that is moved up and down the neck.

(D moved up 2 frets) = E

4th fret			1		2	
5th fret				3		
6th fret			4			

The D pattern is also used with a first finger partial bar.

(partial bar with D at 5th fret) = F

5th fret				1	1	1
6th fret					2	
7th fret			3			

A full or partial bar is used with Am

(partial bar, Am, at 2nd fret) = Bm

2nd fret				1	1	1
3rd fret					2	
4th fret			3	4		

(partial bar with Em at 2nd fret) = F#m

2nd fret				1	1	1
3rd fret						
4th fret		2	3			

The Dm shape ⟨ is usually moved as a **4 finger chord** rather than under a bar.

(Dm moved up 2 frets) = Em

2nd fret			1			
3rd fret						2
4th fret				3		
5th fret					4	

Another 4 finger Dm form that can be moved is the slant with a brace ⋏.

(Dm moved up 2 frets) = Em

3rd fret						1
4th fret				2		
5th fret			3	4		

A variation of this is an upside down V (∧) under a bar, called by guitarists a Major 7th chord. Here it is named by the 5th string bass note rather than by the Dm chord movement.

(Dm under a bar at 3rd fret) = Cmaj7

3rd fret	1	1	1	1	1	1
4th fret				2		
5th fret			3		4	

A 7th chord adds the 7th note flatted to the chord, C7 = C, E, G, + B♭. Major 7 means do not flat the 7th note, Cmaj7 = C, E , G,+ B. To start a fight between pianists and guitarists call the Cmaj7 an Em+4 in the bass, or Em sus.

An Amaj7 (use the same pattern,∧, with no bar, at the 1st fret) can be called a C#m+4 in the bass. This is because a chord requires a certain 3 notes (1,3.5). When there are 4 or more (or 2) notes the question becomes which is the 1, the 3, or the 5. Use the (shortest) chord name which fits with the sound, or the key, or scale progression of the music.

(2) another   Cmaj7

		0	0	0
1st fret				
2nd fret			2	
3rd fret	3	4		

(3) another   Cmaj7

x	x			
5th fret		1	1	1
6th fret				
7th fret					4

(4) another   Cmaj7

	x	x			
7th fret						1
8th fret					2	
9th fret				3		
10th fret			4			

A piano player might play any of 24 possible permutations, or inversions, of the **4 notes** in a Cmaj7 chord using one or two hands:

CGEB   CGBE   CEBG   CEGB   CBGE   CBEG
GEBC   GECB   GBEC   GBCE   GCEB   GCBE
EBCG   EBGC   ECBG   ECGB   EGBC   EGCB
BCGE   BCEG   BGEC   BGCE   BECG   BEGC

Some of these require uncomfortable stretches for a guitarist. The chords and scales in this book are the most convenient to use on guitar.

The purpose of this section is to reveal the way the guitar is laid out by showing the use and connection of 3 major chord patterns (E, A, & C [or D]), and 3 minor ones (Em, Am, & Dm) and 7 major and 7 minor **scale patterns**. These 20 patterns are the foundation of song accompaniment and improvisation. Other musical elements follow or add to the same patterns.

The 7th chords (E7, Em7, A7, Am7, C7, D7 on page 48,) may move up or down the neck with a 1st finger bar and change the same way the major and minor chords do, or they and major 7ths, and other **4 note chords** may not need a bar. Another pattern which moves up and down the neck is the diminished chord: two slants \ \ is one form of it. Wherever it is, it is called by *any* of the four notes it contains.

Diminished Chords:

1)   Edim, or B♭dim, or C#dim, or Gdim

2nd fret			1		2	
3rd fret				3		4
4th fret						

Here is another form. It connects to the one above by putting the 1st finger where the 3rd finger is and repeats the same notes but in a different order:

2)   C#dim, or Gdim, or B♭dim, or Edim

3rd fret				1	
4th fret		2			
5th fret			3		4

This then repeats by putting the 1st and 2nd fingers where the 3rd and 4th are in the #2 pattern then forming the #1 pattern. Diminished chords are used instead of a minor VI. They are a standard part of classic jazz and 12 bar blues. Incomplete or augmented chords give interesting changes and color in music.

Some other fun chords to move and play around with are the: ♭**5+2**, 9th, inside 2, inside 6th, and moving two notes (not a chord) at consistent intervals such as a 3rd or a 5th apart.

x   a   D ♭5+2

	x	a			
1st fret				1	
2nd fret			2			3
3rd fret				4	

(name it by the position of the 4th finger)

(D7+9)   D 9th

4th fret			1		
5th fret	2	2		3	3	3
6th fret					

(name it by the 5th string 2nd finger)

(inside 2)   E2

1st fret			1	
2nd fret		2		
3rd fret				
4th fret		4		

(call it from the E chord position)

(inside 2)   o   A2

			o		A2	
1st fret						
2nd fret			1		2	
3rd fret						
4th fret				4		

(call it from the A chord form)

(inside 6)   E6th   o

					o
1st fret			1		
2nd fret		2	3		4
3rd fret					

(call it from the E chord form)

(inside 6)   x   G6th   o

	x		G6th		o
2nd fret		1			
3rd fret	2				3
4th fret			4		

(call it from the 6th string 2nd finger)

The ♭5+2 and 6th chords move easily as **4 note chords** without barring. **Remember:** If the x,o,a, are not there, do not play the strings that are not part of the chord unless they fit (sound good) with the rest of the chord. Maintain the correct distance when barring. The fingers tend to slide together when moving. There is a full fret space between the bar and the A chord forms (A, A7, A2). If no frets are given assume it is played at the nut in the first position. The names of chords and notes follow in alphabetical order. After each letter there is a sharp (#) **except** after B and E.

3 Major chord patterns
(All E chords)

6 E	5 A	4 D	3 G	2 B	1 E	
			1			1st
	1	1				
			2			2
				2		5th
		2				
	2					
		3	3	3		
						10th fret

3 Major chord patterns
(All C chords, with 7ths)

6 E	5 A	4 D	3 G	2 B	1 E	
					2	1st
			2			
	2		7			
		3	3	3		5th
						7
				1		
	1	1				
				7		12th fret

4 Major chord patterns
(All A chords)

6 E	5 A	4 D	3 G	2 B	1 E	
						1st
		3	3	3		
		4				
4						4
			1			
	1	1				
			2			2
				2		
		2				
	2					12th fret

This is how the chord patterns connect to different positions.

The numbers refer to the chord shape, both major and minor, not to fingers.

1 = a step - ⌐, or backward L, the E and Am form,

2 = slant - / the C, or with a brace ʌ - the Dm.

   (The D form is v or y,)

3 = a strait line - –, the A and Em form.

7 = the flatted 7th note to play in each position to make a 7th chord, and 7th minor.

Adding a flatted 7 © to the Dm shape ʌ in the first position almost sounds like an F chord. Make the Dm7 with the Am7 form at the 5th fret.

3 Minor Chord Patterns
(All Em chords with 7ths)

					1st
	3	3			
				7	2
			2		
	7	2		2	5th
				1	
		1	1		9th
					7

#4 = the form of the G chord (page 44) which is not used except as a G chord in the 1st position. It follows all the A positions this way.

Notice the way the pattern flows. First the step ⌐, then the slant /, (or V or y) then the straight line –, then the G chord form (a check √ that did not bounce) then it repeats with the step ⌐. No matter where a chord is found on the guitar neck - the next position of that chord above and below it is fixed. The scale patterns, which chords are part of, repeat this way too.

Scale Patterns

In addition to chord boxes there is a way to indicate scale patterns. First list the number of the finger for the left hand (the same as with chord boxes). Under that is the number of the fret to press. Under that is the number of the string. Guitarists also write down patterns, other than scales, to keep or practice this way.

Each pattern on the next page provides the least movement with the hand in one (1st, 2nd, or 3rd) position covering 4 or 5 frets. There are no open strings used when playing these scales. The scales are written low note to high, ascending, (Doe, Ray, Me, Fa, So, La, Tee, Doe). Two complete patterns are built beginning on the 6th, 5th, and 4th string. Only one pattern can be made beginning on the 3rd string. They end on the 4th, 3rd, 2nd, or 1st string. No ascending scales can be built from the 2nd or 1st string without stretching out of position.

Notice which position, finger, and string the pattern starts and ends on. If it starts with the 1st or 2nd finger it will end on the 4th, if it starts on the 4th it will end on the 1st or 2nd finger - if it stops or is going to reverse itself. To keep going, up (ascending scale), or down (descending scale), in the same direction, the fingering for the last note(s) may have to be changed where the scale ends and be replaced by whichever finger (1st, 2nd or 4th) begins the next pattern. These are jumps which change the entire position, not jumps within a position.

Scale patterns should become as well known as chords. Patterns may be changed for a particular piece of music or if a person cannot use a certain finger well. For most people the third and fourth fingers of both hands are weak. It may take years of practice before they move well. Keep the thumb in the center of the neck, not over the top edge. Do not hold onto the guitar with the left hand. The decision to use a certain string with a certain finger is made both for tone control and in order to be in the best position to continue without stretching or jumping. These positions allow greatest freedom of movement.

7 major scale patterns
(arranged by string)

Two beginning on the 6th string at the 5th fret: A major scale

1) Finger 4 1 3 4 1 4 1 2

   Fret   5 2 4 5 2 4 1 2

   String 6 5 5 5 4 4 3 3

2) Finger 2 4 1 2 4 1 3 4

   Fret   5 7 4 5 7 4 6 7

   String 6 6 5 5 5 4 4 4

Two beginning on the 5th string at the 12th fret: A major scale

3) Finger 4 1 3 4 1 3 1 2

   Fret   12 9 11 12 9 11 9 10

   String 5 4 4 4 3 3 2 2

4) Finger 2 4 1 2 4 1 3 4

   Fret   12 14 11 12 14 11 13 14

   String 5 5 4 4 4 3 3 3

Two beginning on the 4th string at the 7th fret: A major scale

5) Finger 4 1 3 4 2 4 1 2

   Fret   7 4 6 7 5 7 4 5

   String 4 3 3 3 2 2 1 1

6) Finger 2 4 1 2 4 1 3 4

   Fret   7 9 6 7 9 7 9 10

   String 4 4 3 3 3 2 2 2

One beginning on the 3rd string at the 2nd fret: A major scale

7) Finger 1 3 1 2 4 1 3 4

   Fret   2 4 2 3 5 2 4 5

   String 3 3 2 2 2 1 1 1

Look at all the notes on the guitar on page 46. Notice there are 6 "A" notes (not counting the open A string). The scales on this page begin or end on those notes. One "A" scale connects into the next in a pattern that can be considered a jagged circle (around the outer edge of the neck) or better still, like the lines on a barber shop pole or candy cane that connect and keep going around and around without end. All scales are like that. The diagrams on the next pages illustrate that.

These move the same way the chords do. If you begin ½ step up from A and follow the pattern (keep the same distances between frets and use the same strings) the scale is no longer A but A# (or B♭). Two frets down and the scale is G.

The piano has this all laid out, white keys, black keys, all in a row, though there are patterns to learn there too. The neck of the guitar is, for many, much more of a mystery. The alternative to using chord and scale patterns, is to learn 66 separate chords instead of 6 (3 major and 3 minor) and 154 separate major and minor scales instead of 14 (7 x 2 = 14). Then add to that all the other chord forms and scales possible multiplied by 11. Recognizing patterns helps, even when reading music.

A major Scale patterns

1) 6th string →←

6 E	5 A	4 D	3 G	2 B	1 E	
			1			1st
	1	1	2			→←
	3	4				
4	4					
						12th

2) 6th string ↑↓

6 E	5 A	4 D	3 G	2 B	1 E	
						1st
	1	1				
2	2					
		3				
4	4	4				→←
						12th

A major Scale patterns

→← 7) 3rd string

6 E	5 A	4 D	3 G	2 B	1 E	
						1st
			1	1		1
				2		
			3			3
				4		4
						12th

5) 4th string ↑↓ ↙↗

6 E	5 A	4 D	3 G	2 B	1 E	
						1st
			1			1
				2		2
			3			
		4	4	4		
						12th

A major Scale patterns

6) 4th string

6 E	5 A	4 D	3 G	2 B	1 E	
						1st
			1			
	2	2	1			↑↓
	4	4	3			
			4			
						12th

3) 5th string ↑↓

6 E	5 A	4 D	3 G	2 B	1 E	
						1st
			1	1	1	
				2		
		3	3			
	4	4				
						12th

66

4) 5th string

6(E)	5(A)	4(D)	3(G)	2(B)	
					3rd
		1	1		
	2	2			12th
			3		
	4	4	4		14th

The numbers in the above diagram and in those on page 56 refer to the fingers of the left hand. The diagram above connects directly to the scale on the lower right of the previous page but not to any others. The scales connect without a jump at each "A" note. To move up and down or back and forth, put the finger that starts the next pattern you want to continue with, on the last A of the pattern just completed, instead of using the finger which normally ends that pattern. Sometimes it helps to change position two or three notes before the junction of two scale patterns. Try to play each note clearly. Avoid the temptation to slide into a note except when that is the sound or affect you want.

7 Scale patterns

A major Scale

6	5	4	3	2	1	
E	A	D	G	B	E	
			1			1st fret
	1	1	1)7	7		7
				7		
	1)2	1)2	5)7			5)7
1)2	1)2			5)7		5)7
		2	5)6			
2	2	0.17	5)6	5)6		
		3)6	3)6	3)6		
				3)6		
		3)4	3)4			
	3)4	3)4				12th fret
		4				
	4	4	4			

The numbers here refer to the 7 scales listed on pages 65 - 66.

Have you have ever watched guitarists playing up and down the neck and wondered what they were doing? These patterns are the main highways that are being followed. They are, along with the diatonic scales described on the next pages, the basic tools for improvisation and accompaniment.

Diatonic Scales

A major scale pattern has 2 half steps and 5 whole steps. The pattern is: 1, 1, ½, 1, 1, 1, ½. The C scale is C, D, E, F, G, A, B, C. The half steps are between B & C and E & F. "Dia" means away from. The tonic is the 1, or Doe. Diatonic scales in C are made by using *the same pattern* and **the same notes** but starting and ending on a letter that is not the tonic, C (not Doe of the scale). The Am scales on the right side of this page and elsewhere, are the 6th diatonic scale of C major.

With 7 notes there are 6 diatonic scales. Think of them by number rather than by name. Example: the key of C:

1) C scale begins on C (the 1, Doe, or tonic), it ends on the next higher C (called # 8). Ex.: C to C. This is the *Ionian* scale. (The scales on page 61 are all Ionian in A major.)

2) begin on 2, (Ray) end on 9 of C scale
   D to D, = the *Dorian.*

3) begin on 3, (Me) end on 10,
   E to E, = the *Phrygian.*

4) begin on 4, (Fa) end on 11,
   F to F, = the *Lydian.*

5) begin on 5, (So) end on 12,
   G to G, = the *Mixolydian.*

6) begin on 6, (La) end on 13,
   A to A, = the *Aeolian.*

   This is also the minor scale (the relative, natural, or pure minor).

7) begin on 7, (Tee) end on 14,
   B to B, = the *Locrian scale.*

Minor Scales

7 "A Minor" Scale finger patterns

Two beginning on the 6th string at the 5th fret: A minor scale

1) Finger 4 1 2 4 1 2 4 1
   Fret 5 2 3 5 2 3 5 2
   String 6 5 5 5 4 4 4 3

2) Finger 1 3 4 1 3 4 1 3
   Fret 5 7 8 5 7 8 5 7
   String 6 6 6 5 5 5 4 4

Two beginning on the 5th string at the 12th fret: A minor scale

3) Finger 4 1 2 4 1 2 4 2
   Fret 12 9 10 12 9 10 12 10
   String 5 4 4 4 3 3 2 2

4) Finger 1 3 4 1 3 4 1 3
   Fret 12 14 15 12 14 15 12 14
   String 5 5 5 4 4 4 3 3

Two beginning on the 4th string at the 7th fret: A minor scale

5) Finger 4 1 2 4 1 2 4 1
   Fret 7 4 5 7 5 6 8 5
   String 4 3 3 3 2 2 2 1

6) Finger 1 3 4 1 3 4 3 4
   Fret 7 9 10 7 9 10 8 10
   String 4 4 4 3 3 3 2 2

One beginning on the 3rd string at the 2nd fret: A minor scale

7) Finger 1 3 4 1 3 4 1 3
   Fret 2 4 5 3 5 6 3 5
   String 3 3 3 2 2 2 1 1

A minor Scale patterns

1) 6th string →←

6	5	4	3	2	1	
E	A	D	G	B	E	
						1st
	1	1	1			→←
	2	2				
4	4	4				
						12th

A minor Scale patterns

→← 7) 3rd string

6	5	4	3	2	1	
E	A	D	G	B	E	
						1st
			1			→←
				1		1
			3			
			4	3		3
				4		
						12th

A minor Scale patterns

6) 4th string

6	5	4	3	2	1	
E	A	D	G	B	E	
						1st
		1	1			↑↓
				1		
		3	3			
		4	4	3		
						12th

2) 6th string ↑↓

6	5	4	3	2	1	
						1st
1	1	1				
3	3	3				→←
4	4					
						12th

5) 4th string ↑↓ ↙↗

6	5	4	3	2	1	
						1st
			1			
			2	1		1
				2		
		4	4			
				4		
						12th

3) 5th string ↑↓

6	5	4	3	2	1	
						1st
			1	1		
			2	2	2	
	4	4	4			12th

69

4) 5th string

					9th fret
	1	1	1		12th
	3	3	3		14th
	4	4			15th

7 Scale patterns

A minor Scale

6	5	4	3	2	1	
E	A	D	G	B	E	
						1st fret
	1	1	0.29			
	1	1		7		7
			5)7			
1)2	1)2	1)2	5)7	5)7	5)7	5)7
			6	5)7		
2	2	0.17	5)6			
2	2			5)6		
		3)6	3)6			
		3)6	3)6	3)6		
	3)4	3)4	3)4			12th fret
	4	4	4			
	4	4				15th fret

The A major and A minor scales are used as examples because they begin in the middle of the neck and give an overall view going up or down. Am is the relative minor of C major. The relative minor of A major is F#m.

Look at the major scales on page 78. Each different key will use different notes. With G: the 1, or Doe is G. The notes of G major are: G, A, B, C, D, E, F#, G. Diatonic scales in G use these notes. For the key of G: 1) G to G, the 2) is A to A, the 3) is B to B, the 4) is C to C, the 5) is D to D, the 6) is E to E, (this is the minor scale), and 7) is F# to F#.

It is only necessary to learn the major scale patterns (1st) and the minor scale patterns (6th). With these two as orientation the other diatonic scales are close by and easy to find. The minor scales fit a minor chord progression. Any diatonic scale may work with a major chord progression. Much of the tension and appeal of music results from creating melody lines beginning, or based on, a diatonic scale rather than on the 1 or Doe. The ear is less sure of where the music is going, or when it ends. This adds tension to the music.

70

Finger Picking

The picking code gives the right hand finger(s): T=thumb, 1=index, 2=middle, 3=ring, and the string(s): bass to treble, 6, 5, 4, 3, 2, 1. Movements within brackets [ ] are played together. There are four basic patterns. Once a pattern is learned, vary it, and move it, using whatever strings sound good.

1) Play a G chord with the left hand and use a 4/4 rhythm:
 T-6, 2-2, T-4, 1-3, (repeat 4 times), change to a C chord:
 T-5, 2-2, T-4, 1-3, (repeat 4 times), change to a D chord:
 T-4, 2-1, T-3 (or 5), 1-2, (repeat 4 times), change to a G chord:
 T-6, 2-2, T-4, 1-3, (repeat 4 times), end.

2) 3/4 time, one bass string alone, then 3 treble strings played together:
Use a G chord, repeat, C chord, repeat, D chord, repeat, end on G.
(G) T-6, [1-3, 2-2, 3-1], [1-3, 2-2, 3-1], T-4, [1-3, 2-2, 3-1], [1-3, 2-2, 3-1],
© T-5, [1-3, 2-2, 3-1], [1-3, 2-2, 3-1], T-4, [1-3, 2-2, 3-1], [1-3, 2-2, 3-1],
(D) T-4, [1-3, 2-2, 3-1], [1-3, 2-2, 3-1], T-5, [1-3, 2-2, 3-1], [1-3, 2-2, 3-1],
(G) T-6, [1-3, 2-2, 3-1], [1-3, 2-2, 3-1], T-4, [1-3, 2-2, 3-1], [1-3, 2-2, 3-1].

3) Single note, 6/8 time, played evenly, or emphasize a certain note(s):
(G)　T/6, 1/3, 2/2, 3/1, 2/2, 1/3,　T/5, 1/3, 2/2, 3/1, 2/2, 1/3, (repeat)
(Em) T/6, 1/3, 2/2, 3/1, 2/2, 1/3,　T/5, 1/3, 2/2, 3/1, 2/2, 1/3, (repeat)
©　 T/5, 1/3, 2/2, 3/1, 2/2, 1/3,　T/4, 1/3, 2/2, 3/1, 2/2, 1/3, (repeat)
(D)　T/4,　1/3, 2/2, 3/1, 2/2, 1/3,　T/5, 1/3,　2/2, 3/1, 2/2, 1/3,　(2x, end on G).

4) One bass and treble string together and a regularly alternating bass.
(G) [T-6, 2-2], 1-3, T-4, 3-1, T-6, 2-2, T-4, (repeat),
© [T-5, 2-2], 1-3, T-4, 3-1, T-5, 2-2, T-4, (repeat),
(D) [T-4, 2-3], 1-2, T-3, 3-1, T-5, 2-2, T-3, (repeat),
(G) [T-6, 2-2], 1-3, T-4, 3-1, T-6, 2-2, T-4, (repeat, end).

The individual finger strokes for the right hand are like moving a diving board or a trampoline. Press the string into the guitar, then roll off it, letting it spring back and vibrate. Plucking it outward, or up and down strokes, does not give the clearest or loudest sound. To get maximum volume, or to emphasize a note, raise the finger higher and dive into the string - do not pull it. Mute or stop a string's sound with the base of the hand or the base of the thumb.

How to Practice

This is an intermediate level book. The reader should already have some experience with learning songs and making music. The sound of a major scale, Doe, Ray, Me, Fa, So, La, Tee, Doe, perhaps from the song "Doe A Deer," should be well known. The diagrams of the chords and scales show where to put the finger(s) and what string(s) to play. It can not get much simpler than that. **Just do it**. Greater understanding will come *after* the chords and scales have been played and the attempt to move them has been made. Read the prayer on page 18.

The right hand finger movements and finger picking can be tried in songs now. The main principle of this book is that just a few (20) patterns can be moved up and down the neck to make most of the basic chords and scales. Learn these 20 elements by heart. *First* try to master the (3) **major**, and (3) **minor chords**: the step ⅃ (E, Am), the slant / ©, Dm) [or y (D)], and the line – (A, Em), **in all three positions**. Move them as **bar chords** to make different major chords. Play them in **chord progressions**. *Next* learn the (7) A **major scale patterns**. Move them to play other major scales (try: C, D, E, & G,). *Then* learn the (7) A **minor scale patterns** and move them also (try: Bm, C#m, Em & F#m). *Finally* try the other diatonic scales.

It is not an exaggeration to say each element must be practiced 1,000 times before anything else can be done with it. That is: 20 times a day for 50 consecutive days. The "A major" and the "A minor" scales given are a complete description of all the patterns. Learn each one, then connect it to the ones next to it. Go back and forth between two scale patterns, then three, then connect 7 of them covering the entire neck of the guitar in one key. Listen to the practice of other instrumentalists and vocalists. Everyone practices scales. Scales can be as well known as chords.

Not all scale patterns are needed in each key and they are not all convenient to use while playing. The head or the body of the guitar gets in the way. Leave out the A major scale beginning on the 5th string which moves below the 12th fret. Use it only for practice in that key. That pattern is useful when playing in the key of G, (begin on the 5th string at the 10th fret) or E, (7th fret) or D, (5th fret) or C, (3rd fret).

The tension of a major scale always resolves to its tonic, the 1, or Doe. When the scale gets around to Doe again the sense is that it is finished, stop. To overcome this feeling, in order to keep going into another scale position change the **beat** and play with the **rhythm** as well as with the scale or melody. The minor scale and the other diatonic scales <u>do not</u> give the sense of stopping on Doe. Instead the feeling is that they can continue forever. When practicing minor scales use the rhythm to get a sense of when to stop.

First use a slow, steady 4/4 beat: 1-2-3-4, 5-6-7-8. Rhythms are often given by syllables. Three quarter time can be thought of as: bumpity, bumpity, bumpity..., end-on-a bump. Work with the 3/4 beat: 1-2-3, 4-5-6, 7-8-7, 6-5-4, 3-2-1, 2-3-4, 5-6-7, 8. Add 8-9-10 to keep going up. Turn back with 14-15-14. Triplets allows you to cover one or more scales twice before ending. Broken triplets can continue without ending: 1-2-3, (back one) 2-3-4, (back one) 3-4-5, (back one) 4-5-6, 5-6-7, 6-7-8, 7-8-7 (returning) or 7-8-9 ascending. Another way is to emphasize certain notes: **Bump,** adity, bump, bump, bump, bump, = 1, 2-3-4, 5, 6, 7, 8. Count to yourself.

The scale patterns rotate on the neck like the stripe on a candy cane. There are only 3 (or 4) different ranges or octaves. To get an idea of what notes are available around each position, play some of the notes outside the pattern that are easy to reach without changing position. Connect each scale to the chord in that position. Think of the scale as a song all by itself. Practicing scales helps in all types of music. If they are learned well it will be easier to play corded-lead or pick out a melody.

The information in this book does not make advanced guitar playing easy, just easier. It may help to have a teacher to work with but time and effort are still required. Not everyone will want to learn all 20 elements and 4 finger picking patterns. The creative use of the scales comes as a surprise to some people. Ideas just "pop" out after months of practice. "Accidents" are also a source of creativity. Others use a knowledge of music theory to integrate more chords and scales into the music they make. What it means to want to play "better" is different for each person.

Some musicians can "hear" in their head what they want to accomplish and just follow the sound once they learn how to make it. Still others learn by imitation of pre-existing music. "Play Bach" is very good advice. Simple pieces such as the **C maj. Prelude,** or the **Em Bourke**, or **Jesus, Joy of Man's Desiring,** by J. S. Bach, (Segovia, or Foster guitar transcriptions) lead the hand through all three positions, moving chords and scales, over the entire neck of the guitar.

After playing something 1,000 times you may get sick of it so try not to use up your favorite songs or pieces for practice. Here are some ideas to try **_after_** the chords and scales are learned by heart.

1) Record yourself playing any typical chord progression. Play each chord   in each of three positions four times (3 X 4 =12):

      I, (12 times), vim, (12x), IV, (12x), V, (12x) slowly, (all 20 times).

(example) ©   (Am)   (F)   (G)

2) Play along with it using all or just certain notes of that scale or play a melody. Stay in that key. When the chord changes, play the diatonic form of that scale: the 4 under the IV chord, the 6 under the VIM, etc.. Diatonic scales do **not** have to go with just a certain chord but this is an easy way to help hear where the chord changes come in.

3) Do this in 5 keys. A, C, D, E, and G.

4) Tune the strings up to pitch with a tape, or CD, or internet download and play along using the scale.

5) Take turns with a friend, first one plays the chords while the other plays the lead, using the scale patterns, then switch roles.

6) Play along in church. <u>You must be able to hear your own guitar</u>. When the worship gets loud it is easy to use the wrong chords and scales.

7) Read and play the notes from guitar sheet music. Learning one or two Baroque pieces will cause the hand to travel over the entire neck, using most or all of the chord and scale patterns. Play Bach.

More Music Theory

Major Chords

A major chord is made up of 3 notes, the 1, or Doe of a scale, plus the 3, and the 5 note of that scale. The C chord of the C scale (below, and on page 66) is made up of: **C**, (1) **E**, (3) and **G** (5). The order these are played in, (called inversions) or which is in the bass, middle, or treble, may change: **C,E,G, C,G,E, E,G,C, E,C,G, G,C,E, G,E,C**. They are each still a C chord.

A chord may be played on the guitar using 3 bass, middle, or treble strings, or any combination of strings. The other strings may add color (a different note that sounds good), or repeat any of the 3 notes, or be silent. Each chord can be easily played using a different fingering at 3 different positions on the neck of the guitar: first (near the head), second (middle of the neck), or third position (near the body of the guitar). The first position then repeats after the 12th fret (on longer necks).

Major Chord Progressions of Songs

```
        1   2   3   4   5   6   7   8   (Arabic numbers for notes)
C scale = C  D   E   F   G   A   B   C
        I   II  III IV  V   VI  VII VIII  (Roman numerals for chords)
```

A typical chord progression uses the: I, IV, V, & minor VI. To **transpose**, or to change the key, find the number (I to VIII) of each chord of a song, and then replace with that same number from a different key.

7 progressions →   I   IV   V   VI minor

(This is how a song is   1) C   F   G   Am   5) G   C   D   Em

easily transposed from   2) D   G   A   Em   6) A   D   E   F#m

one key to another)   3) E   A   B7   C#m   7) B   E   F#   G#m

                      4) F   B♭   C   Dm

A minor II, or minor III, and other variations are sometimes used. The symbol for a minor chord is a small m after the capital letter or after a sharp or flat (Em = E minor, C#m = C sharp minor, B♭m = B flat minor).

Minor Chords

A minor chord uses a: 1, 3, and 5, of the relative minor scale (see page 69). It may instead be considered as being made of the: 1, 3, & 6, of the major scale it is related to.** Am is made up of: **A, C, & E**. To make a major chord a minor, flat the 3, (move it ½ step down). The A chord is: **A, C#, & E**, Am uses: **A, C, & E**. The C chord is: **C, E, & G**, Cm is: **C, E♭, & G**.

Minor Chord Progressions

Typical minor chord progressions use: I minor, IV minor, & V7 of a minor scale (a flatted 7th note added to a chord = a 7th chord [V7]). A II7, a Vm, and a VI7 are alternatives to the 6 possible variations in each key. Ex:

Progressions →	Im	IVm	V7		Im	IVm	V7
1)	Am	Dm	E7	5)	Em	Am	B7
2)	Bm	Em	F#7	6)	Fm	B♭m	C7
3)	Cm	Fm	G7	7)	Gm	Cm	D7
4)	Dm	Gm	A7	*Solm	Dom	Ré7

Both major and minor progressions usually end by returning to where they started, the I, or Im, chord.

*Minor scales and chord progressions are often associated with the music of Middle-Eastern or Latin cultures. Many of these countries use the Sofage method instead of letters to indicate a note: C = Do, D = Ré, E = Mi, F = Fa, G = Sol, A = La, B = Si, (Fa#m, La7, Do♭,).

** To be consistent with accepted music theory, some prefer to label the minor progressions according to their relation to the major scale. The order of a major scale is: I, II, III, IV, V, VI, VII, VIII. The minor scale begins on the VI (6th diatonic) so the order for it is: VI, VII, VIII, I, II, III, IV, V, VI. Thus: the Im, IVm, & V7, would be called: VIM, IIm, and III7. Both ways work as long as you are aware of what system is being used when you share chords with other musicians.

Music Scales

Our music system uses 12 tones or notes. The distance between each note is called a half step. The capital letters A B C D E F & G are used to label musical notes. The symbol # (sharp) placed after a letter raises it ½ step. The symbol ♭ (flat) after a letter lowers it ½ step. The distance between each fret on a guitar is a half step. After the 12th fret the notes repeat. Beginning with C the 12 tones are:

C, C#, D, D#, E, F, F#, G, G#, A, A#, B.

It then repeats the same notes but in a higher range: C, C# D, D#, and so on. Notice that after each letter (note) the next note is a sharp **except** between E & F, and B & C, which are only ½ step apart (1 fret on the guitar). There is a whole step (2 frets on a guitar), between all the other letters. One whole step is made up of two half steps. C to C# is ½ step apart (1 fret), so is C# to D. C to D is 1 step (2 frets) or two half steps apart. The 12 tones can be written using flats (♭) instead of sharps (#):

C, D♭, D, E♭, E, F, G♭, G, A♭, A, B♭, B.

There are some differences between sharps and flats but when playing a note they are equal: C# = D♭, D# = E♭, F# = G♭, G# = A♭, A# = B♭. Sharps are written when moving up a scale and flats when descending. It is in the context of the written music that the difference is noticeable. Guitar music is often written, as much as possible, with just sharps, when needed (the key of F almost always has a B♭). For the purposes of this book the sharp and flat keys are not used as examples. The guitar can play in any key but certain ones are more comfortable or allow a greater range, freedom of movement, or tone.

A demi-tone scale (half tones) uses all 12 tones, each note is ½ step apart. Playing each note of any one string on the guitar produces a Demi-tone scale. On the E string that is: (open) E, F, (1st fret), F#, G, G#, A, A#, (or B♭), B, C, C#, D, D#, E. A major scale uses just a certain 8 notes, in a particular pattern, out of the entire 12 tones. It begins and ends on the same letter but the last note is considered a higher octave. The first and last are the same letter. An 8 note scale only has 7 different notes or letters.

There are other scales as well. To learn how to use them we begin with the major scale which has 7 letters (8 notes).

Some Major Scales

	Doe	Ray	Me	Fa	So	La	Tee	Doe
	1	2	3	4	5	6	7	8
C scale =	C	D	E	F	G	A	B	C
(steps or pattern)	1	1	½	1	1	1	½	
D scale =	D	E	F#	G	A	B	C#	D
E scale =	E	F#	G#	A	B	C#	D#	E
F scale =	F	G	A	B♭	C	D	E	F
G scale =	G	A	B	C	D	E	F#	G
A scale =	A	B	C#	D	E	F#	G#	A
B scale =	B	C#	D#	E	F#	G#	A#	B
C scale =	C	D	E	F	G	A	B	C

Major scales can be made beginning with any of the 12 notes. Examples are usually given in the key of C, a C major scale, because it is the only one that has no sharps or flats. Arabic numbers are used to indicate a note of a scale (1,2,3,4, etc.). Roman numerals are used to indicate a chord of a scale (I, II, III, IV, etc.).

Notes	1	2	3	4	5	6	7	8
C scale =	C	D	E	F	G	A	B	C
Chords	I	II	III	IV	V	VI	VII	VIII

Minor Scales

There are 3 minor scales. The basic one is the:

1) Relative minor (also called the pure or natural minor), it is related to a major scale. It begins on the 6th note of the major scale. Example: C D E F G **A** B C, "A" in the C scale. Am is the relative minor in the key of "C". The relative minor scale uses the same pattern and notes as the major scale it is related to. The difference is it begins on the sixth note of that scale and ends eight notes (an octave) higher on the 13th.

Example of a relative minor scale:

```
 1   2   3      4   5   6   7    8   (9   10   11   12   13)
 C   D   E      F   G   A   B    C  =  C major scale
   1   1   ½   1   1   1  ½   1   1   ½   1   1
 Relative minor (Am)  =  A   B   C   D   E   F   G   A
                        1   2   3   4   5   6   7   8
```

2) Harmonic Minor - the pattern is: 1, ½, 1, 1, ½, 1&1/2, ½. Between the first note and the second note is one whole step, (which equals two half steps) the next note is one half step away, then one, and so on. An example of the harmonic minor: A B C D E F G# A.

3) Melodic Minor - the pattern is 1, ½, 1, 1, 1, 1, ½. An example, of the melodic minor: A B C D E F# G# A

A melodic minor scale works going up, ascending, but the sense of it gets lost going down, descending, so the natural minor is used going down.

Some Other Scales

A Whole tone scale uses 6 notes, each note is 1 step apart, example:
C, D, E, F#, G#, A#, C.   or   A, B, C#, D#, F, G, A.

Another 6 note scale is the Blues scale. The pattern for the Blues scale is: 1 and ½, 1, ½, ½, 1 and ½, 1 (1 and ½ = 3 half steps or 3 frets).
example: C, D#, E#, F#, G, A#, C,   or   A, C, D, E♭, F♭, G, A.

A Pentatonic scale uses 5 notes. The pattern for the major Pentatonic is: 1, 1, 1&1/2, 1, 1&1/2. Ex.: C, D, E, G, A, C. or, A, B, C#, E, F#, A. The minor Pentatonic: 1&1/2, 1, 1, 1&1/2, 1. Ex.: C, D#, F, G, A#, C. or, A, C, D, E, G, A. These are associated with oriental music.

Music Notation For Guitar

The written form of musical sounds has included the use of shapes, colors, letters, the Sofage, (Doe, Ray, Me, Fa, So, La, Tee, Doe), pictures of an instrument indicating what the fingers should play, and **the 5 line treble staff**. The notes on the staff lines are: **E, G, B, D, F**. Some people remembered this by, "Every Good Boy Does Fine." Notes in the spaces between the lines spell out: **F, A, C, E**. Above and below the staff the notes follow in alphabetical order: the space below the bottom line **E, is D**, the line below that is **C**, (middle C). The E below middle C is the low E (6th string) on the guitar. The space above the top line **F, is G**, the line above that is A, and so on. The next high E is the sound of the 1st string of the guitar pressed down at the 12th fret. The notes on the guitar neck are shown on page 56. The theory of a chord is given. Major and minor scale theory is in this book too.

The time to hold a note, or let it sound, is also given with notes. A whole note is an empty circle. A note that is half dark is a half note which is held half the time, or is 1/2 as long as a whole note. A solid black note is a quarter note, held 1/4 as long as a whole note. Four 1/4 notes = one whole note. A quarter note with a line or flag attached is an eighth note 1/8 (♪), with 2 lines it is a 16th, with three it is a 32nd, etc...

The key signature at the beginning of the music tells what sharps or flats (what key) to use and also gives the rhythm or meter (4/4, 2/4, 3/4 or others). When no meter is given the music is in 4/4 time. Adding a sharp or flat to a note effects that note every time it occurs on that line. A natural (♮), means ignore the sharp or flat instructions for that note, on that line. Two dots (:) at the end of a line mean repeat the line. A block (▬) on a line is a rest, silence. There are other symbols as well, some for specific instruments. Music literacy is usually gained by one or two years of piano study. It is easier to learn it that way than by working with a guitar or other instrument that usually requires two hands to sound a note.

Guitar sheet music usually includes the fingering for the music. A small 1, 2, 3, 4, beside the note indicates which left hand finger to use. The letter a, m, i, (from the Latin for: index, middle, ring) usually above the note, indicates which finger of the right hand to use on the treble strings. The bass strings are almost always played with the thumb. A number 1 to 6 in a circle indicates which string to use. A Roman numeral on top, III, V, VII, etc. means use the first finger as a bar or partial bar at that fret. The bar is held until other direction is given which requires letting go of the bar, or hold it to the end of a string of dots. For instance 1/2IV......┐ means hold the three treble strings down with the first finger at the fourth fret, playing all the notes indicated, with the hand in that position, using whatever other fingers are required or indicated.

If there is a piece of written music you want to learn, buy it and begin. The above information should be enough to get started if you can already play somewhat. The chart of all the notes on the guitar is included on page 46 of this book. How to find them, is on page 67. If the music does not have guitar fingering on it you will have a lot more work to do.

On piano music these symbols may mean something else. Music for a specific instrument usually has tips on playing, written for that instrument, with its own special code. It helps to be able to read music but this is not the only way, or even the main way, to learn to play the guitar.

The first two sections of part II of this book described how to play by patterns, not by reading music. First, there are the chord patterns, and how to move them. Then, there are scale patterns, and how to move them. Then, more music theory is given which you may, or may not, want to read first. I put most of the music theory at the end of the book because many guitarists do not use it. If you find it confusing just follow the patterns. Learn the **3 major chords**, and how to move them, the **3 minor chords** and how to move them, and the **7 major scales**, and the **7 minor scales**, and how to move them. Learn the 4 finger picking patterns and change them as you wish. The information given on what chords are, and what scales are, may be understood better after you play and hear them often. Other scales and chords can be learned later too.

Sideways Movement and Labeling Chords

The chord shapes can also be moved sideways, along the width of the neck, as well as up and down the neck lengthwise. Moving these shapes sideways is not the best sounding or most convenient way to make these chords. A fourth note is often needed. These diagrams are included to reinforce the concept of moving shapes or patterns and to help label chords. It can be difficult to name a chord. **Not all positions are chords**. All examples are at the first fret.

the step ⌐

B　　　x　o　o

	1	
2	3	

o　**E chord**　　o

		1
	2	3

a　o　Am

		1
	2	3

x　x　x　C#aug

			1
		2	3

G7　*o*　o　a

	2	
3		4

the slant /

x　　**C Chord**　　o

		1
	2	
3		

x　a　Dm

			1
		2	
	3		4

x　x　x　D#7

			2
		3		4

Em2　o　o　o

1	2	3

o　B7 ? E sus4 ? o

1	2	3

the line —

a　o　**A Chord**　o

1	2	3

x　a　a　F#m

	1	2	3

A major chord has a 1,3,&5 note of a major scale. To label a chord treat each note as if it were the 1. Try to find the other notes of that scale. If they are not there then it may not be that chord. Treat each as if it were the 3, then the 5. Use the shortest name that fits best. The 1, 3, or 5 are not always played or known. If you add a note, or move the 3 & 5, it changes the chord's name. When you flat a note (or chord) it moves down ½ step [diminished]. Sharp a note moves it up ½ step [augmented]. Here are some general rules: to follow. Do not label a note a flat or sharp 1 or 2. A 2 note can be added. A flat 3rd =a minor chord. A sharp 3rd = a 4th (a.k.a. suspended). Do not call a note a sharp 4th, call it a flat 5th (♭5). Adding a sharp 5th makes an augmented chord, do not call it a flat 6th. A real 6th can be used. A sharp 6th = a flat 7 note. An added flat 7 is called a 7th chord. Adding a real 7th is called a major 7th chord. A sharp 7 = the 8th.

A 9th or a 13th are notes added in a higher octave. Notes can be added in the base, middle, or treble part of a chord. All the notes in a diminished chord are 1&1/2 steps apart. The key of a song, or the sound, feel, or purpose of the chord, help determine the name. Diatonic chords are made by using notes in only one key. For the key of C some diatonic chords are: C, Dm, Em, F, G, Am, and G7. These chords have no notes that are not in the key of C. These, and inversions, play corded lead. The inversions are: 1,3,5 - 1,5,3 - 3,1,5 - 3,5,1 - 5,1,3 - 5,3,1.

Review

Read the first section. Practicing, or even making music, is not the same thing as worshiping the Lord with music. Do all to the Glory of God.

To practice, first: Learn the 24 elements, and how to move them.

3 major chords: *E, A, & C,* / **3 minor chords:** *Am, Em. & Dm* , / **7 major scale patterns**, / **7 minor scale patterns**, / **4 finger picking patterns**.

Play the chords, and scales, and transpose songs, into 5 keys: A, C, D, E, G. Practice with songs, with a CD or tape, an Internet download, or with someone else.

Suppose you want to play a hymn with a corded lead. You may be able to find the notes written out on a treble staff for a guitar, or you may try to work it out from a Hymn book written for piano. Go for it. If you have an ear for music, know the melody of the hymn, and you know the scales and chords in all three positions on the neck, and you know finger picking, and how to emphasize a note, you can figure out the song yourself, arrange it, (memorize it with fingers and mind), and play it without reading notes. Pick a key, one you like to play in, and/or one that fits your voice range for the song.

  C   G   C

Just As I am without one plea, (Begin with a C chord in first position. The first three notes are: the C on the 2nd string, the D on the same string and the E, of the open first string. All are easy to reach. The other notes in the melody, thus far, are also easy to reach, before, during, or after, the chord changes.)

          F   C

But that Thy blood was shed for me, (The note for "was" uses the F chord but it is higher, and easier to reach in the 2nd position [D shape played at the 5th fret],)

               F

And that Thou bidest me come to Thee, (The melody moves higher, use the second position)

  C   G   C

Oh Lamb of God I come, I come. (Back to first position, but what picking do you use overall? What scale portions connect sections? base, middle, or treble strings? Your choice!)

About the Author

John Jay Frank has led worship and actively spread the Gospel through songs at: high schools, colleges, prisons, assisted living facilities, nursing homes, hospitals, hospices, in parks, and at music festivals, and over the radio, TV, and the Internet, as well as in all kinds of Protestant and independent churches (including some Catholic groups). He studied classical guitar at the Brooklyn Conservatory of Music and at the State University of New York at Cortland. He learned to play banjo (barely) using a book and studied the piano (but never did learn to play) in Indiana, Ohio, and France.

In addition to **A MINSTREL'S NOTES** he wrote a book for pastors and church counselors and others interested in the field:

MYTHS, LIES, AND DENIAL:
Christian And Secular Counseling In America

and the book,

TURNING BARRIERS INTO BRIDGES:
The Inclusive Use of Information and Communication
Technology for Churches in America, Britain, and Canada

and produced three CDs of his own songs:
For All God's Children
Comfort Ye My People
The Cross Of Life

and three CDs of:
Hymns of God's Grace
Hymns Of The Church
Hymns And Carols

and a DVD,
Pick'n and Preach'n, rom performances
filmed in Connecticut and California

Contact minstrelmissions@gmail.com See www.minstrelmissions.com
* * * * * * * *

**All of this and all to come is laid at the foot of the cross.
To God Be the Glory!**